DIVINELY ALIGN ME

Titles by Alicia Young

DIVINELY ALIGN ME

HOW *Signs* FROM THE *Universe*

KEEP YOU ON YOUR PATH

᠑

ALICIA YOUNG

PARASOL PRESS

Asheville, USA, and Adelaide, Australia

Publisher's Cataloging-in-Publication Data

Young, Alicia, author.

Divinely align me: how signs from the universe keep you on your path / Alicia Young.

Includes bibliographical references and index.

Asheville, NC: Parasol Press, 2022.

LCCN 2022900364

ISBN 978-0-9965388-7-9 (pbk.)

ISBN 978-0-9965388-8-6 (ebook)

LCSH Omens / Signs and symbols.

BISAC Body, Mind & Spirit / Unexplained Phenomena.

BISAC Body, Mind & Spirit / Angels & Spirit Guides.

LCC BF1777 .Y68 2022

DDC 133.3—dc23

PARASOL PRESS

Australia: PO Box 7029, Hutt Street, SA 5000

United States: Asheville, NC 28805

Email: **info@aliciayoung.net**

aliciayoung.net and soulplans.net

IG and FB: @authoraliciayoung

TW: @IamAliciaYoung

Cover design by Shruti Diwan

Cover specs by Sally Jaquet

Interior design by Tessa Avila

Cover art licensed by CanStockPhoto, © denbelitsky

Author photo © Grier Neilson

Printed in the United States of America and Australia

First printing 2022

10 9 8 7 6 5 4 3 2 1

For Laura

WHO IS ATTUNED

Contents

Preface

The Universe is asking you to dance.

As it bows gently before you and extends its hand, a choice is presented.

You can decline and remain a wallflower . . .

(The Universe prefers not to plead, nor will it demand that you acquiesce. It respects your free will.)

. . . or you can willingly partner for a riveting choreography that is your life.

It is *always* your choice.

If you accept, you know the dance won't be seamless. In fact, stumbles are guaranteed. It's all in how you perceive those missteps: as blunders that make you withdraw or dissolve into peals of laughter, or as a gateway to doing better and immersing yourself more fully. And that makes the collaboration all the more beguiling and trusting and significant.

Over time, we see our dance cards fill. We might long for the smooth glides and elegant twirls of a waltz in an old black-and-white movie, but where is the growth or adventure in a lifetime of that? Some days will be infused with the jubilant looseness of hip-hop. And we've all experienced a jarring segue into heavy metal (jarring, that is, unless you love heavy metal), more suited to a sweaty mosh pit than a ballroom.

Sometimes it will seem like the Universe is taking the lead, and it's all you can do to keep up. Other days, you will strike out with your own moves, confident and in synch with the music. If you're playing it safe, you might just be handed a dramatic dip or a spotlight solo to keep you on your toes.

And you know how it feels when someone cuts in!

Regardless, the beat transports us.

Why now? Why explore signs and their roles in our lives?

There's a shift playing out, and it's internal.

Our lives have changed in recent years on almost every level, and for the most part, we have met this change with reactions that are positively feline in their swiftness and grace. The pandemic has claimed lives and livelihoods, and it has divided families. (Conversely, it has also been a springboard for compassion and more closely knit communities, as neighbors check on one another.) Add to this the racial reckoning that has unfolded across the US and around the world, and the ever-present backdrop of climate change, and you have a volatile cocktail of stressors. Mask protocols, devastating wildfires, and widespread protests have taken up residence in our thoughts, conversations, and daily lives. Underpinning this all is the impact on global economics.

All this change swirling around has invited an unprecedented level of introspection—a wholesale accounting of who we are, what we want out of life, and if we're on course to get there. Is it enough to see family through a phone screen? Is it time to re-evaluate work? Is it too late to change careers, to pursue a sea change or tree change? Many of us feel prompted to re-examine a slew of choices as to how we spend our time and energy.

Given this, can you think of a better time to tap into the magic around us? I believe the Universe is waiting to reveal the beauty in seemingly random occurrences. And in turn, those events are infused with meaning. They could hint at new opportunities, or guide us to release a relationship or to stand up more vocally for our beliefs.

As routines unravel, it's only natural that we can feel unsettled. That's when I began thinking more about signs. They can appear in a reassuring way that helps steady our footing, providing a firm grip on a handrail.

Signs can awaken something already within us, from a gentle stirring to a near-seismic shift. We all have an idea in mind as to how we want our lives to be—but then we think, speak, or act in ways that undermine this vision, whether wittingly or unwittingly. We sync our devices, but we can forget to synch our internal GPS to the outer world. We're all aware of the digital recognition in the invisible network of Wi-Fi. I picture something similar with people.

When we don't pay attention, the Universe amps up its message. It lovingly persists in repeating the same type of sign, or delivering them with more intensity, to ensure we get the message.

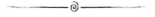

My family is from India, and I grew up in Australia. I am one of nine children and was introduced to the idea of angels right along with solids. I became a social worker, then a broadcast journalist. Throughout, I have long been drawn to spiritual topics, but this fascination stayed in the background during my years in news. Over time, it became more pressing.

I had a few spiritual experiences, which I later realized prepared me for the main event. I had an OBE (out-of-body experience) in which I met the soul of a little boy. Bobby was the unborn son of my close friend Jane. He had a loving message for his grieving mother, and I was no more than a go-between. I was permitted to watch one of Bobby's pre-birth soul-planning sessions, in which he chose his parents, his siblings, and even his birth order. I recount this transformative experience in my book *Visit from Heaven: A Soul's Message of Love, Loss & Family*. It pivoted me from the headspace of news to the heartspace of soul plans.

Signs at their core are magical and mystical, and small signs can be just as meaningful by reminding us of our connection to loved ones. I recall strolling through Manhattan a few years ago when my nephew Flynn came to mind. I smiled to imagine him growing up to live in New York, a man-about-town in the city that never sleeps. Moments later, I gasped as I turned the corner to see a sign several stories high: The Flynn—Coming Soon! It was an ad for a luxury apartment complex, and the artwork showed a man wearing a tailored suit, with the wind in his hair. Signs speak to our hearts, not our logic.

Years ago, I contemplated penning a book on either Audrey Hepburn or Jackie Kennedy. Around that time, I met up with my sister in Manhattan, and we found ourselves staying with Jackie's former housekeeper. What were the odds? Anne Marie Huste hosted a walk-up boarding house in the Murray Hill neighborhood. Eventually, I wrote about how to tap your inner Audrey in a rushed world, but the sign I received around a book on the former First Lady was nonetheless a tantalizing morsel that whispered "maybe."

PS: A word on words. Where I reference God, Universe, Source, or Spirit, please know I am referring to the same consciousness. Likewise, terms such as heaven, the afterlife, or the Other Side reference one plane of existence. Feel free to mentally insert your own language around these concepts as we go through.

And while we're on the topic of terminology, pardon me while I coin a new collective noun: a *resonance* of signs. After all, signs most often appear in a sequence of synchronicities, and this series catches our attention, resonating with our heartspace even as logic might dictate otherwise.

Introduction

As it turns out, it *is* all about you—in the most divine way.

Your spiritual growth.

Your divinely designed plan.

Your joyful purpose (your gift to the world).

You arrived here, but your arrival was not in isolation or independent of others, and neither is the life that has revealed itself since. You are part of a tapestry of humanity. The Universe celebrates your essence in all your glorious imperfection.

I'm sure you have held a newborn and wondered, "What does the world have in store for you?" I believe that little one, so poignantly innocent and defenseless, houses a soul of infinite wisdom. Before birth, that soul mapped a plan for its upcoming life. And it's through signs that the Universe lends a helping hand with our soul plans, providing support, encouragement, and direction as needed.

As you read the experiences in the following chapters, especially those of lifesaving protection, you might ask why one person was protected and not another. I ask that you consider the outcome from the perspective of soul plans, in which we plan our entry point (our family and culture, for example) and our exit point for our upcoming life.

What Is Alignment?

I believe that our alignment flows from a sense of spiritual equilibrium, when we feel that even keel between our internal and external lives (some days better than others).

Alignment is a sense of being in flow with our current circumstances and with the path we're walking. It doesn't mean that life is pain-free, but you knew that already. Nevertheless, it does give us a more centered inner core to tap. I don't think we are leaves blowing around in the wind at random. I believe there is a divine, intricate plan for each of us, and it's our spiritual task here on earth to discover and embrace it. When we tap into our joyful purpose, we are in alignment. We know with quiet certainty that we are exactly where we are meant to be at a given moment, through celebrations and challenges alike.

Alignment whispers rather than bellows. Alignment is most easily *felt* rather than plotted on a screen or mapped out in rigidity. It leaves space for a little magic to unfold. Imagine going on holiday to a new destination. If you schedule and coordinate every minute of your itinerary, there is no chance for spontaneous adventure.

What Are Signs?

Serendipity. The word itself—how it feels on my tongue—is enough to make me smile. Serendipity and signs are close cousins, both being tools of the Universe to help us along our way. They each elevate an experience of happenstance, imbuing it with more meaning.

Just as street signs help us cut through a maze to our destination, metaphysical signs help guide our path through life. By their very nature, signs need to grab our attention before they can suggest a direction.

What are the odds? These four little words chime in like an operatic refrain to help us discern signs when they appear. When a seeming coincidence presents itself, it jolts us into awareness of the remote chance a given event might ever happen. *What are the odds?* As we think it or say it out loud to others, we give ourselves pause to process hidden meaning in an apparently random occurrence.

Universally Accepted Signs

Signs show up in myriad ways. They might take a classic form, such as feathers or coins in unusual spots, or a song that we associate with a loved one in spirit. Many of us are attuned to recurring numbers. Signs can also adopt a decidedly human form: enter the earth angel. Many of us have experienced a person who pops into our lives, seemingly at random, to pose just the right question at just the right time. Their presence pivots us in a fresh direction or equips us with an unexpected perspective. It's like that old saying, which I believe holds a lot of truth: *people come into our lives for a reason, a season, or a lifetime.*

Feathers and butterflies are widely considered messages from loved ones and from the angelic realm in general. Many people have shared that clocks have stopped at the moment their parent or grandparent passed. Friends or relatives in spirit can signal they are close by through meaningful songs, whether through specific lyrics or because those tunes were a favorite of theirs.

Dragonflies are seen to herald support amid transformation, be it personal, professional, or spiritual.

There is another, less easily discernible sign. An apport refers to a physical object that mysteriously appears in order to ease our heartache or comfort us in some other way. In later chapters you will read about a crystal that appeared on the bed of a grieving daughter who lived alone, and a pair of glasses that were left behind at a wake but later reappeared in the widow's home. Neither item had a logical explanation.

What Purposes Do Signs Serve?

Essentially, signs keep us aligned to the plan for our life that we designed before we came here. But signs never dictate: they simply point the way to get us back on course, then encourage us to keep going. I don't necessarily mean a dramatic correction, but perhaps a tweak. Ships can change course by a few degrees and arrive at an entirely different location.

Signs in the early stages of a romance can be especially telling. I will long recall a woman who found herself floating in euphoria when her crush finally asked her out. One afternoon they stopped by his parents' home to pick up something, and the sneering way this man spoke to his mother sparked a shift inside the woman. She suddenly saw this scenario as her future dynamic with him. That might sound presumptuous, but it rattled her.

Signs can serve as a loving wake-up call. As a gentle prod (or a pressing need) to forgive. Common, but nonetheless useful, physical signs of fatigue or illness can signal a need to slow down and pay more attention to our health. It might be as subtle as a sniffle or as debilitating as a migraine.

Signs might also reveal themselves as a nudge to set boundaries or to maintain our existing boundaries. Setting personal limits can present a particular challenge when they involve a passion of ours, be it a volunteer position or a new grandchild. The push-pull of our enthusiasm versus the other hats we wear in life offers a wonderful chance for growth and balance.

Signs can infuse courage by the truckload or just enough for a given moment, like a careful sprinkling of a pungent spice.

Signs can provide a playful jolt to shake us out of our routine and reconnect us to the magic we knew as children. On a recent evening walk, I noticed a small group of people gathered by the beach. A seal was frolicking in the water, and locals were delighting in it. I saw that no one was whipping out their phones to film her: they were simply immersed in her antics. It gave me pause, and I was drawn to their faces. Their expressions were soft; their eyes smiled; and their foreheads were relaxed and unfurrowed by stress. As they began to peel away, they spoke in subdued tones, almost reverent for the show that Mother Nature had gifted them. I am certain that the next time those people returned to the beach, they would reconnect to that experience and look for the seal again.

We can become so focused on going through the motions of daily life that we lose sight of the wonder around us. While a healthy skepticism has its place, if we lapse into cynicism it can begin to calcify around us; it needs to be chipped away like barnacles on the side of a boat.

We've all heard of a vicious circle. Why not a joyful circle? When we open ourselves to magic, it ushers in a spiritual calibration.

Choosing to Be Open to Signs

When major events occur in our lives, some of us will take them on face value while others will feel propelled to discern their deeper meaning. We have multiple lenses by which to view the world and our place in it. Signs are simply one way, but a powerful way. And like so many parts of our human experience, they involve a choice: a choice to entertain the possibility that signs exist and show up for a reason.

Sandy F. from Australia was visiting extended family in Michigan when they were involved in a fatal crash. She was a passenger in a car that ended up not only on the wrong side of the highway but facing the wrong way.

In the aftermath, she would have to contend with severe physical repercussions, including abdominal and head injuries. And the larger meaning was not lost on Sandy. She reflected at length as she recuperated. She believed the accident—and the position and location of the car—were clear signs to both slow down and change direction in her life. She had been dealing with a toxic work environment and a relationship that did not honor who she was. When she eventually returned home, she changed jobs and released the relationship.

Misconceptions about Signs

Many of us carry unwarranted assumptions about signs.

Signs exist for a select few. On the contrary, signs are available to you whether you're a priest or a prisoner, a show girl in Vegas or an aid worker in the Sudan. An Islamic proverb declares that "every blade of grass has its own angel, willing it to grow."

In other words, the Universe is whispering words of encouragement, championing even the most minute speck of life to become what it was destined to be. I delight in that sentiment.

We can't ask too often for signs. As if there exists a monthly limit or lifetime quota! The Universe is a place of limitless abundance. Ask away.

We can't ask for too much—or for material things. We come here to experience the physical world, and material support can ease stress and struggle amid the pressure of modern life. Asking for a sign that you will receive job security or a bit of extra cash is not only permissible, it is lovingly welcomed.

We can't ask for trivial things. Whether you're searching for your keys or a life partner, you are worthy of receiving help from the Universe.

I don't deserve it. Beloved, you are assuming you must deserve help in order to receive it. You exist. That is enough.

I'm not religious. Does that mean atheists can't get signs? (I ask with a smile). The Universe does not judge.

It's lazy. It's a slippery slope. No one is advocating a dependence on signs. We don't need to abdicate our responsibility or agency in life.

You needn't maintain a constant vigil to look out for signs, as if in the jungle with binoculars and a pith helmet. Trust that signs will find you. Signs can show up in the most discreet ways. Conversely, they can feel like a slap so startling you can almost feel your cheekbone shatter.

The Big Picture—and Your Place in It

Jung spoke of synchronicity as deeply meaningful coincidence that occurs mysteriously in life. He also subscribed to the concept of Unus Mundus, meaning "one world." Jung believed in a realm where everything is connected, whether through seen or unseen means.

You might have heard of the Net of Gems (aka Indra's net) in Buddhist and Hindu cosmology. Each jewel is said to radiate such beauty and clarity that it reflects facets of all others around it: what a delightful way to consider our interconnection.

Dr. Bernie Beitman studies coincidence and likewise endorses the idea of an unseen tapestry. His fascination began as a child when his dog ran away. Young Bernie got lost while searching for his pet and took a wrong way home—only to find his dog along that unexpected route.

Adulthood delivered another seminal moment in Dr. Beitman's life: one night at home in San Francisco, he suffered an apparent choking incident at his kitchen sink—only his throat was clear. This frightening ordeal occurred around 11:00 p.m. The next day, a sibling called with the sad news that their father had died from choking. He had passed at 2:00 a.m. in Delaware, which is 11:00 p.m. on the West Coast. Did one thread in the universal tapestry pull on another?

The Intimate Picture: Your Plan

The Universe acknowledges the peaks and troughs of your human experience and applauds your decision to join in by arriving here for this lifetime. You genuinely are a brave soul.

As the cosmos sends you on your way, it does so like a parent sending a child to camp: it encourages your efforts to grow and stretch into new experiences. It wants to help—and it *does*—but also knows you will learn more if it simply takes a step back. It ladens your backpack with a compass, a mud map, hearty fare for sustenance, and a few treats for comfort. (We speak of "manna from heaven" for a reason.)

You use these tools to navigate your journey. And when you find yourself wandering from your path, signs appear to realign you, to nudge you back on course. It's a divine back-up system, whether deploying a subtle course correction or a sharp hairpin bend.

Signs so often appear to help us through transition—because change can be scary, even when we want it. There's the kind of change that we choose (to study, to travel, to start a business) and the kind imposed on us (a parent remarries, a company downsizes). Signs of encouragement or reassurance that all will end well can be a life raft in choppy waters.

You do not need to earn signs; they are your birthright. Let me joyfully remind you: you exist, therefore you are entitled to celestial support.

The Universe has at its disposal every imaginable way to convey a sign to you. The full spectrum of the natural world is at its fingertips, from the animal kingdom to every tree that stands and every river that flows. It can summon every lyric to every song ever written (including ones you've composed in the shower) or your personal catalog of childhood memories. This ensures a tailored sign resonates for you, from an ancient adage to the most fleeting of pop-culture references. Consider your favorite holiday as a child, or your first day of school, or a movie scene you can recite verbatim. Each image, mood, and moment can be called on.

The Role of Intuition

Just as the Universe has everything at its disposal to send a sign, you can use everything at *your* disposal to sense and interpret it.

Your physical senses are a great first filter: ask anyone who has caught their mother's perfume wafting by or felt a brush on their cheek in the days after losing a loved one. Your body is a prime instrument for receiving messages at a visceral level.

Yet, if you rely solely on your five senses to interpret the world around you, your perceptions would be limited. You would miss out on the power of harnessing your intuition. You might call it a hunch or perhaps an inner voice, but regardless, you have been honing yours since infancy. A newborn, far from being verbal, is finely attuned to the vibrations of the room.

It is often said that feelings are the language of the soul. When something feels right, we know it, whether that means a new person in our life or our first impression on walking into an open home. We draw on our intuition far more than we acknowledge.

There are libraries of books that explore dreams and their rich symbolism; aren't signs symbols in our wakefulness? In our sleep state, we let our guards down, and messages can better reach us. Perhaps we need signs to cut through the daily distractions . . . messages that grab our attention and penetrate our consciousness.

The Role of Patterns

If you've ever found yourself drawn into a crime-series marathon, you know that a fingerprint needs a minimum sequence of matches to be considered acceptable or admissible in court. It's often the same with signs. Some stand alone and pack a punch, but often we need a sequence to feel clarity around a message.

Conversely, some signs stand out for doing the exact opposite. You might remember a game from *Sesame Street* called "One of these things is not like the other." We were taught early on to spot similar items and group them together. By default, the thing that seemed out of place caught our attention; anomalies often serve as signs.

The Gift of Curiosity

From quilting to quidditch, curiosity raises our antenna to explore. Curiosity is a little like flirtation. In flirting, we're not saying yes or no, but offering a playful "maybe." This extends far beyond people. I flirted with law school, for example, and quickly found it was not for me. Do I regret trying it on for measure? Not a chance. The pleasure is in the discovery, the possibilities. I was grateful that the signs showed up so early and clearly that I didn't spend a year or more mired in indecision. The experience played a role; it still washed over me and shaped who I am today. It broadened my thinking.

Gratitude

I think I was born with an extra dollop of gratitude. That probably sounds like an odd claim to make. You wouldn't put it in a résumé, or mention it at a cocktail party, or include it on a dating profile. ("I enjoy long walks on the beach . . . and feeling grateful.") But it's there. Maybe it stems from growing up in an immigrant family who had it especially tough those first few years, or from watching my parents selflessly toil at jobs they would not have chosen. I feel gratitude every time the light bill arrives, and we can pay it in full. When I was growing up, my parents settled many accounts in partial payments, chipping away every month, and that has stayed with me always. When I became a journalist in local news, I had good days and bad like anyone else. But I always knew that there would be a line around the block for my job, and I can genuinely say I was grateful every day.

When a sense of thankfulness flows through us—whether a fleeting appreciation for a small kindness, or something much stronger and deeper—it travels far and wide. I believe the Universe acknowledges gratitude with love, which in turn creates more love. Others witness it and perhaps are inspired to be more thankful, and so it goes and grows.

Gratitude for signs of love and support not only opens portals in our hearts and minds, it keeps the channels free to receive more guidance from the Universe.

It completes the circle: Asked. Received. Acknowledged.

Signs help reveal:

The wonder that is you.

The soul that is you.

The gift that is you.

I have long believed in signs, from wherever they arise in the Universe: from our angels, guides, distant ancestors, loved ones in spirit, or Mother Nature herself. Let's delve deeper.

PART I

Signs

FOR SPECIFIC NEEDS

CHAPTER ONE

Protection

We used to joke that my father needed so many angels, there would be mass unemployment in heaven when he passed.

As I look back on the stories you're about to read, I'm a little embarrassed at the number of times I've been protected. It implies that I barrel through life recklessly. In fact, that's not the case, nor did it apply to Dad. But I have to consider that a free spirit, and a reasonably traveled one at that, would encounter a few situations that called for extra help. These days, I'm more grateful than embarrassed.

My Experiences

Meeting My Guardian Angel at Age Three

As mentioned, I'm one of nine children. We would pile into the car (in the days before mandatory seatbelts), and my sister and I would roll around in the back. At red lights, drivers would point and count, slack-jawed at the number of heads and limbs crammed inside.

One afternoon, we were returning from a day out, when my parents made a final stop. They hopped out to visit a store, with our oldest sister left in charge. I still don't know how I emerged from that entanglement of limbs, but I followed my mother and father and was about to scurry across the road.

I was stepping off the curb when I felt a tug on my shoulder, pulling me back from the brink. Wheels screeched, and horns blared. As I spun around, I looked up into the eyes of a beautiful old man. His smile radiated kindness, and his face was weathered by sun and age in a way I now realize gave me a lifelong affection for those features; it was joy and wisdom etched into the lines of his skin.

I spoke with no filter, as young children do. "You're my guardian angel," I announced, as if it were mundane. He nodded, smiled, and faded. I was then swarmed by grown-ups.

Decades later, I still feel both the fascination and the acceptance of that moment.

One Seat in Four Hundred

In college, I answered an ad for a roommate in a house across the street from campus. I had been taking six buses each day, and it was wearing me down. I was excited to think how much time I would save—and yes, how late I could sleep in. I arranged to meet a guy straight after my morning lecture.

I often arrived early to class to get a good seat. But that day, I seemed to be running through wet cement. I was dismayed to see the lecture hall packed, with only a few vacant spots dotted across the cavernous room. I began shuffling in one direction, then another, only to be blocked each time by someone else. That left one seat all the way on the far side.

As I sat down, two students in front of me caught my attention with their animated chat. Their friend had also called about an ad for a roommate. The man had locked the girl in a room, threatened her if she left, and marched around the perimeter of the property in army fatigues. It had taken her hours to escape.

He was the same man I was due to meet an hour later.

Rabid Dogs at the Leprosy Hospital

I volunteered at a leprosy hospital in India years ago and arrived after dark. A woman on staff explained the way to the ward the next day. "Be careful," she intoned. "There are two stray dogs on the property, and we're certain they have rabies." I cringed; a childhood incident with a dog still haunted me.

The next morning, I was walking along a dirt path when my knees went weak. I heard them before I saw them: two mongrels, snapping and drooling as they bounded toward me. I was startled at the words that came out of my mouth: "Thank you, God, for protecting me." Not "Would you?" or even "Could you?" but expressing thanks in advance.

What happened next will stay with me forever. No sooner had the words come out of my mouth when both dogs stopped barking. They slowed down and ambled along for a little while before losing interest altogether.

I couldn't wait to phone my Auntie Grace, a nun, who promptly scolded me. "You asked for protection—you got it—and then you questioned it!" she said, but she couldn't mask the delight in her voice.

Zimbabwe: Angel in the Rapids

Years ago, my husband and I took a trip to Africa on a shoestring budget and signed up for whitewater rafting. Jon is a lifelong surfer and a strong swimmer. Photos show him smiling casually, while I am frozen in fear.

We approached a severe rapid, the water violent. The next moment, I found myself flying overboard. Within seconds, my helmet peeled off, and the raft seemed miles away. My body and spirit were in direct contrast—my limbs were flailing desperately, yet my mind was completely calm, and I found myself thinking, "This is it. This is how it ends." I called out to my guardian angel.

Immediately, a man appeared on a rescue kayak. He led me into calmer waters, though the current was still thrashing about. Soon, I was scooped out of the water by another group of tourists, who hauled me onto their raft.

I was still shaking with relief hours later when I was reunited with Jon. Our group faced a steep climb back from the lowest point of the rapids. Everyone else grumbled, but I was full of gratitude to have my feet back on terra firma.

A Human Trafficking Tip-Off

Many signs are a joy to recall, though occasionally one makes me shudder. Even then, I'm soon awash in relief for how differently things might have turned out.

For a time, I was based in Kolkata, doing volunteer work at a hospice run by Mother Teresa and her Missionaries of Charity. In my early days there, a series of synchronicities evolved that I believe saved my life. Among the volunteers was a group of religious brothers who seemed stitched together in a long-practiced routine of seminary life: rising at the same time, attending communal prayers, and catching trams en masse to their shared workplace.

That morning, a brother—known for his punctuality—was uncharacteristically dragging his feet. This meant he lost the group, and in playing catch-up, he overheard a seemingly random conversation on a tram that proved critical to my safety. He was horrified to hear the men mention an Australian girl who was staying at the convent. He quickly realized it was me they were discussing. This man was aware of human trafficking before the phrase was widely used. He was also in a position to fast-track that information, as he had a friend in the police force. When I returned home that night, my aunt (the nun) summoned me. She told me she had been visited by the religious brother and his detective friend. Apparently, I had been noticed on the street outside the convent for my paler skin and (modest) Western clothing. It was not uncommon for women to be forced into prostitution, and rumors were surfacing of a white sex-slave ring; the paler the victim's skin, the more money her controllers could demand. "At least she's too old to be sold into marriage," the detective had said, trying to be helpful. (I was twenty-eight.) I absorbed this development in silence. I had seen the headlines, watched news reports, and discussed trafficking in my social work course—but never had I heard my name mentioned in the same sentence as a prostitution ring. I had traveled with the brothers my first few days in town, and they offered to accompany me again. I gratefully accepted.

Taxicab in Chile

Let me tell you what happened a few years ago when we didn't heed a sign. I share this not to be alarmist or to imply that ignoring a sign will invite disaster, but to underscore the need to honor our intuition.

Jon and I had moved to a small town in Chile, a few hours south of the capital. We didn't live locally full-time, but rather based ourselves there as we came back and forth from work assignments elsewhere. Whenever we returned, we tended to nest at home, but we also wanted to explore the country.

We booked a B&B in the seaside port of Valparaíso and were excited to explore. It was mid-afternoon, and we had no sooner checked in when we headed out again for a walk. We found ourselves winding through the hills. Students were ambling home from school, and *abuelitas* (grandmothers) sat in their front yards, sunning their legs. This peaceful image began to change as the neighborhood became sketchier. I murmured a prayer to Archangel Michael to keep us safe. Out of nowhere, a taxicab appeared around a corner; we were taken aback, as something about it seemed oddly out of place. Perhaps it was a little too modern or sleek for the area.

I'm embarrassed to tell you this, but we ignored this obvious sign (which literally provided an escape) and went on our way. Minutes later, we were held up at gunpoint. It all unfolded in seconds; we heard shouting behind us, and as we turned, we were jumped by three young men. The shortest, who looked to be about fifteen years old, began pulling at my bag, which I had worn across my body. Amid all this, I realized that Jon was awfully quiet.

As I turned to my left, I saw two older youth, perhaps eighteen or nineteen, one with a gun to Jon's head. The other boy had a broken bottle to my throat. Jon's voice floated up so calmly and gently. "Just give them everything," he said. "Just give them everything. . . ."

I've often thought how differently it all could have been had we simply jumped into that cab. It emphasized for me the need to trust my intuition.

Signs Shared with Me

A Future First Responder

My Auntie Grace was a nun for more than seventy years, and she shared some experiences with me when I stayed at her convent in Kolkata many years ago. It was one of my favorite parts of the day, sitting with her by the lamplight and talking quietly.

This first experience occurred while she was a mother superior and school principal in the hills of Kurseong, near the tea plantations of Darjeeling. Close friends of hers had recently welcomed a baby boy, and she made the journey down to their apartment in the city. She described their home as a loving one, but also quite loud—a stark contrast to the serenity of the convent. For this reason, it was memorable that she found herself alone with the infant in his room. She turned away to get a diaper and turned back to see a majestic angel standing over his crib, with its wings spread.

Auntie Grace told me he was about eighteen feet tall, and that his head went through the roof, yet she saw it easily. She couldn't find her voice. She explained that this celestial being had no clear outline, as he was made of soft gold dust. They talked, she said, "but not the way we do, with our mouths." Instead, their communication was by thought. The angel explained to her that this child would always be protected. This presence seemed in no hurry to leave, and Auntie estimated she could have counted slowly to fifty before he eventually faded.

This baby grew up to become a first responder, so this early sign of protection was no doubt a comfort to his parents and family.

The Power of a Name

When a young woman becomes a nun, she adopts a new name in place of the one bestowed by her parents. Often it will combine the names of saints or holy figures to whom she feels a special connection.

This was the case for my aunt. While born and raised as Grace, she became Sister Mary Aquin: Mary, for the Virgin Mary, and

Aquin, for Saint Thomas Aquinas. In those days, the religious sisters rarely visited their family homes. This was both to cut costs and to emphasize that the church was their new family and focus. Over the years, it became a novelty to hear her childhood name. (I can relate. Alicia is actually my middle name. Whenever I hear my first name these days, I suddenly have a major flashback: I am ten years old and in big trouble. . . .)

As I shared earlier, Sister Mary Aquin was the principal at a school for orphans, as well as a mother superior. From time to time, she would be approached by one of the more affluent members of the community, offering to fund the repair of a sinking roof or perhaps, as on this occasion, to throw the children a party. She happily accepted.

On the appointed day, the children were besides themselves with excitement. There were games, sweets, and gift bags galore. Little girls discovered treats such as hair ribbons and dolls; little boys delighted in slingshots and toy soldiers (it was the 1960s). When it was time for lunch, they sat down to a feast. Food was served on banana leaves, as their custom dictated. Sister Aquin was bustling around when she heard someone calling "Mother," but something else needed her immediate attention. Again, she heard a voice calling "Mother," this time with more urgency. She told herself she would finish this task and then tend to what was needed. Suddenly she heard *"Grace!"* in a stern, loud boom.

She swung around, startled to hear her childhood name. No one was there. But before she could process that, her eyes were drawn straight to the leaf placed in front of a small boy. It was not a banana leaf. She swept over and pulled the child away, examining the fare spread out. It was different from the others and had a dab of paste that was later found to be poison. The police were called, and the "benefactor" eventually admitted guilt. That particular day was the feast day of the goddess Kali, and the woman had intended nothing short of a child sacrifice. The little boy was critically ill, but survived.

Girl, Interrupted

This experience was shared with me years ago by a person we'll call Frieda.

Frieda was backpacking through South America in the early 1990s. She was in Peru when an ad for a bus tour caught her eye. She stopped by a travel agency to leave a deposit and told the woman she would return to pay the balance. The agent was friendly and chatted about the local sights.

When Frieda returned, she was startled to find the woman refused to accept her balance on the trip. Her demeanor had starkly changed, and she was rude and abrupt. She thrust the deposit back into Frieda's hands, and all but pushed the young woman out the door. Frieda was mystified, but it was clear she would get no explanation. Shortly after, she turned cold as she saw the news reports: a terrorist group had hijacked a bus, raping all the women aboard and shooting dead all the men. Frieda would have been on that bus with them.

Let's cast a wider net now, to see how signs show up amid diverse backgrounds and circumstances.

Others' Experiences

A Protective Bubble

What began as a drive to the country one Saturday turned out to be more than just a leisurely outing. My mother was visiting from overseas, and we had planned a scenic drive to show her the magnificent Australian outback. I was the front passenger, my partner the driver, and my mother sat in the back. As we were driving along remote gravel roads, I started to feel uncomfortable about the speed we were going, and I urged my partner to please slow down. Unfortunately, he continued and not long after that, he lost control of the car. We were careening straight for a tree at more than 50 mph.

I felt everything in slow motion. I could feel the car spinning out of control and flipping onto its side (I was on the bottom). It was at this moment when I noticed I was completely encircled in what felt like a clear bubble, and a voice said to me, "You will be all right." Throughout the whole incident, I stayed calm and still, just waiting for the car to stop. I had no fear, nor worry. My mother was calling out my name from the backseat, frantic. Finally, the car came to a halt, with the tree snapping at its base. It pierced the side of the car, missing my leg by a fraction. It all felt surreal, more like I was a bystander than a participant.

A farmer on a tractor suddenly appeared. He helped us climb out of the smashed car and drove us to the pub in the nearest town to rest and to contact family. People were astounded that we had all walked away in one piece; I know without a doubt that it was divine intervention that kept me safe.

—*Susanne Pearce, PhD, Adelaide*

A Decision That Saved My Life

I have always had a feeling surrounding decisions, whether they are right or wrong, or possibly dangerous.

I am Australian and was working in England as a teacher's aide when I was twenty-two. I lived in a hostel with four girls in a cramped room. I wanted to move out, and two friends who lived in a lovely flat asked me to move in, as one of them was leaving. I had the strongest feeling that I had to either stay in the hostel or leave England to go home to Australia. My friend kept asking me, "Do you want the room or not? It's exactly what you have been looking for." I told her that if I moved out of the hostel, I had to go home. She argued that didn't make sense. After ignoring a feeling earlier in the year about taking a job (which turned out to be a terrible choice), I decided to go home—a big decision!

The night after I arrived home from the UK, I was watching the news with my family. There on the screen were images of the London bombings. The tube line that I would have caught to work was one of those that got bombed, at about the time I would have been on the train.

—*Alicia Geddes, Melbourne*

A Trio of Signs

I was raised Catholic, and whenever I stopped at a church in my travels overseas, I always lit a candle for my loved ones. This particular time, I was in San Diego visiting a friend when I discovered a lovely church. As I went in and knelt down, I felt a full-body tingle, as if I had been touched by an angel. I will never forget it.

Another time, I was in London and using a rideshare to get home after a night out with friends. I'd had a few drinks and felt a bit of flu coming on, so I wasn't the most clear-minded. I began dozing off. Suddenly, I realized that the driver wasn't taking me home; we began heading down dark streets in a different part of town. Immediately, I knew I wasn't alone; I sensed "the whole team" of angelic protection around me. I felt emboldened and told him to get me home. I was unquestionably protected.

And in Broome, Western Australia, we lived in a rough part of town known at the time as "The Bronx." The house had shutters that would stay open, offering scant protection. The area was sketchy, and burglaries were common. I sensed otherworldly protection, and I believe I had two sentinel guardians posted outside.

—*Fin James, energy alignment mentor,*
Denmark, Western Australia

Angelic Voices

I had just graduated Penn State, but my first husband was a year behind me, so we remained on campus in cramped quarters. At the time, I had a lot of fear around death and had been searching for a sign that God exists.

Our apartment was so small, the bed was close to the hallway door. I was lying on the bed, resting but not sleeping (I suffered insomnia), when I heard a man call my name. I sat up, certain that someone had broken in; it was so clear and close by. A moment later, feeling the panic rise in me, I heard three angelic voices. They were young and female, and they sung a chord (not a line of a song). I will remember it always. I felt so safe.

—*Annette Y., Santa Fe, New Mexico*

Shine a Light

It was the 1960s in the jungles of Sri Lanka, and my son was a baby. My husband was overseeing the ground-clearing of five thousand acres for a tobacco colonization project. Conditions were rustic, and our home was powered by a generator a distance away. Each night, staff would signal with a flicker that the electricity supply was about to be shut off until morning. We were simply too isolated to receive visitors.

It was astonishing, then, to look up one afternoon to see my Uncle Joe walking toward us. To our delight, he had decided to surprise us with a visit. He had taken a long and winding bus journey to our nearest town, and then hitched a series of rides before completing the final stretch on foot.

We were showing him around when we came to the baby's room. Something made me look up to the ceiling. I was puzzled; there seemed to be an extra wire at the light above our son's crib. We began to peer closer, but at that moment the generator cut out, and we were plunged into darkness. We had no light to better see what it was, when Uncle Joe produced a pen light from his pocket.

The "extra wire" was a snake! It was the same green color as the light wire and had coiled around it. I shudder at what might have been, with that snake dangling over the crib.

To think: An unexpected visitor showed up in such isolated surrounds. He had the exact thing we needed, at the exact moment we needed it. Our baby was protected.

—*Lourdie and Astor, Koondoola, Western Australia*

Help Sent

I had enjoyed a weekend with my best friend and was waiting to catch the bus for the ten-hour return trip. I heard ambulances wailing. Whenever I hear a siren, I usually ask the angels to help whoever is in pain.

I felt a strange uneasiness, and I prayed to keep calm ahead of the long overnight journey. I sent healing energy to all my loved ones. By the time I boarded, I was feeling a little better, but the eeriness persisted. We stopped for dinner, and I called my parents. My mother answered her mobile phone and told me she was out with my father. It was unlike them to be out late.

When I arrived home, I was shocked to see my father had lost two front teeth, with lacerations on his lip and a dislocated thumb. My mother suffered bruising to her elbow and knees. I froze.

The night before, Dad had lost control of his motorbike amid light rain. Bystanders called an ambulance, and my parents survived what would have otherwise been a horrific accident (the location was notorious for buses and trucks hurtling by at high speed). All this transpired while I was waiting at the bus stop more than more than 300 miles away!

I had no idea what to do. I petitioned the ascended masters to lead me. Though in shock, I followed the clear but short instructions I received:

- *Call Karla* (my friend, a dentist). She immediately visited my father and monitored him for weeks. She also put me in touch with a senior dentist. Dad soon had dentures, and his smile returned.
- *Go bring the bike back with Gautam* (my neighbor and close friend). By chance, he was home, and he took me to the accident spot. The bike was in good condition, and I rode it back.

- *Bring fruits and medicines.* I picked up all I'd need to help my parents heal.

I could not process anything at that time, and I merely followed the instructions of my inner voice.

—*Shruti Diwan, website developer, Perth*

Divine Light Protection

My husband and I were enjoying a holiday through Europe and the UK. At one point, we found ourselves in Edinburgh, Scotland. Two memorable things happened that day.

First, in the afternoon as we were crossing the Waverley Bridge, I was overwhelmed with a feeling of being surrounded when there was no one else around. "Can you feel that?" I asked my husband, Darren. "Can you feel all the energy around us?" He shrugged. I felt uneasy, but we still headed to a ghost tour. After all, Edinburgh is known as the City of the Dead.

The tour included a visit to a former prison where an active poltergeist was said to reside. While I was curious, I wasn't about to take any chances; my anxiety levels were rising. I asked archangels and spiritual guides to surround me in divine white light. We entered the cell, with a dozen of us crammed in like sardines. It was pitch black, and the smell was musty and putrid, but as we stood there shoulder to shoulder I felt peaceful and protected. Suddenly, an uneasy energy passed by, but I remained calm. The two women on either side of me fainted and had to be carried out. I believe the divine white light cocooned me. I thanked Spirit for protecting me that day.

—*Maria Bowes, intuitive massage therapist, Adelaide*

CHAPTER TWO

Guidance

*A*ncient explorers were guided by the stars. I believe signs are the modern metaphysical equivalent of constellations.

Whether you're a planner at a cellular level or more of a free spirit, you will occasionally find yourself at a crossroads. Perhaps it's an issue at work or you have reached an impasse in a relationship, unsure how to proceed. At these intersections, you might welcome guidance in whatever form it takes. A sense of direction can infuse stability amid tumult. Signs don't replace decision-making. They can, however, point you in the right direction with a cosmic sleight of hand. You still need to make the call and own it.

You have an intricate divine plan, designed in loving collaboration with the Universe. Any plan requires steps, with the opportunity to move forward or to choose from multiple options.

Some people believe that in a perfect world, you'd never question your path, finding it early and following it diligently. But I believe beauty lies in the false starts and stumbles. You might begin in one direction, and then a situation arises, or a question is posed that pivots you along a different route entirely. That's when even the most adventurous among us can crave a little guidance or a dose of reassurance that all will be okay.

✿ My Experiences

The following trifecta of signs played out to guide and reassure me in publishing my first spiritual title, and nudge me to the next title, which you're reading now.

A Light Bulb at Sunset

It was a balmy summer evening, and Jon and I strolled to the beach to watch the sunset. We fell into comfortable silence, and as I dug my toes into the sand, thoughts turned to my book *Visit from Heaven*. I cherish the out-of-body experience that prompted it, but I also knew that its spiritual nature could upend my career in news. *Is this a good idea?* I silently asked my guides.

I glanced up and was startled at how quickly and clearly they answered. At that precise moment, the setting sun looked like the top of a light bulb (the international symbol for an idea), and its reflection formed the bottom half. (You can see a photo of it online at **soulplans.net** and **aliciayoung.net**.)

A Sweet Sign on Christmas Day

In Australia, Christmas Day is often celebrated at the beach. Jon and I had recently moved to Adelaide and didn't know many people. We planned a simple picnic to enjoy the outdoors. That morning, however, we slept in. We delighted in homemade cards from our nieces, Livinia and Annie, and opened some gifts but didn't linger over them. Among them was a book from Jon's parents. I slipped it into a bag and planned to look at it after lunch.

We enjoyed a decadent spread. As Jon headed off on a short walk, I settled in for a chat with the Universe again about *Visit from Heaven*. Though I was delighted to see it published, I still hesitated to go public about my experience. I was struggling.

Should I speak about this? Writing the book had stretched me enough; doing interviews was another bridge. *Send me a green light,* I implored. Even as I said it, I laughed; what did I honestly expect to happen on a semi-remote beach? I imagined a giant traffic light plummeting from the sky with its emerald button lit up and dismissed the whole thing with a smile.

I rummaged around the bag, and found the book Jon's parents had given me. It was a funny, quirky offering: *Behind Every Successful Woman Is a Substantial Amount of Chocolate* by Suzy Toronto.

As I turned to the first page, my eyes fell on this passage:

> *So, there you go . . .*
> *it's a green light,*
> *a legitimate excuse,*
> *PERMISSION FROM GOD*

Consider that. First, that I had received a book on such an unusual topic. Second, that I had asked specifically for a green light and then, moments later, found that exact reference in a book . . . on confectionery. And further still, to see it followed by written, divine "permission." What are the chances? It resonated as a powerful sign of guidance—and on Christmas Day, no less.

Soul Publishing

Two years after receiving the light bulb sign, I was considering another spiritual title (this book!) and wondered: *Should I focus on spirituality full-time?* Again, the Universe was quick and agile in its response.

We had headed to wine country for a relaxing winter getaway, courtesy of my sister and brother-in-law. It was time to unplug, read, and chat away the hours. I was talking to my angels, asking if I should step away from the headspace of news to the heartspace of soul planning.

I glanced up and saw the spine of a coffee table book, which read "Soul Publishing." I was shocked. And intrigued. The book was not at all spiritual; it was about regional wines! Soul Publishing was the name of the company. Let me add: it's rare to see the publisher's name spelled out on a book spine. Usually, it's simply a logo.

Sign sent. Message received.

And more signs have played out around my job, as you will read below.

Spanish School

My sister and I were in Playa del Carmen, Mexico, for a week. It was a relaxing mixture of Spanish classes and a chance to loll about. One afternoon I found some quiet time, lying in a hammock and talking to Spirit. I was at a crossroads in my career, wondering if I should leave broadcast journalism. The idea left me desolate; I relished interviewing people, writing news stories, and voicing the scripts. That said, the sheer competition of television news could be draining. I asked for a sign on whether to keep going.

I got up and headed to the computer room, which was usually packed with fellow travelers posting updates home. Strangely, I was the only one there. I had barely sat down when the receptionist popped her head in the door. "Hey!" she called out. "Do you know anyone who could voice a video for our website?"

It was a sign of reassurance delivered minutes after I had asked for it. I remained in journalism and went on to adventures in Russia and South America, to name a few.

Walter Cronkite

We had recently moved to Houston for my husband's job. As a trailing spouse, I was used to gearing up to find work in new settings where I knew almost no one—and certainly no one in my field.

I began cold-calling television and radio stations, then moved on to local production houses. It was disheartening, but I kept going.

A few days later, I decided to approach my job search a different way. I would make a vision board of how this next chapter would look, and then ask my angelic guides to run with it. I sifted through magazines and collected pictures of friendly gatherings, homes, symbols of spirituality, and female public speakers, but couldn't find images of journalists. I believed that if I could meet someone in the industry and show them my work ethic, they might help me open doors. I finally found a picture of Walter Cronkite, who, of course, was a news legend known for decades as the most trusted man in America.

Two weeks later, I called a production house and had barely begun my spiel when the man interrupted me. "Can you come in right away?" he asked. His executive producer had resigned moments before in the wake of a family emergency. Minutes later, I was in his office, and he was briefing me on a health documentary. I had been a medical reporter and a hospital social worker, and I was hired on the spot. As he left, he added, almost as an afterthought, "Oh, and it's being anchored by Walter Cronkite."

It was a powerful reminder that while we might consider an outcome impossible, the Universe does not.

Dr. Deepak Chopra

Jon and I were staying near La Jolla, California, one Thanksgiving. It's a scenic and charming seaside town.

We were enjoying a long, meandering walk, each lost in thought; I was calling on my celestial friends about speaking more on metaphysical topics. (I still felt the tug between news and spirituality.) My imagination can run away with me at times. I could join a speaker roster with Oprah or Deepak Chopra, I thought. (A girl can dream!) I then looked up to see a man walking toward us. He seemed oddly familiar, yet we knew no one in this town. *It was Deepak Chopra himself.* I was stunned, but not too stunned to say, "Sir, I very much respect what you do" without breaking stride. I was dying to stop him but couldn't bring myself to intrude. Dr. Chopra smiled and nodded in thanks. He was gracious. Our interaction was momentary, yet I will remember it always.

It was a clear sign of support to keep going.

The Green Light from Mrs. Schrock

Mrs. Schrock was our next-door neighbor and a fixture of my childhood. I would perch on her orange vinyl kitchen stool and read to her. I could feel her love well before I could articulate it. Sometimes she would take me on errands. Once we went to a weight-loss meeting; she was so excited she declared, "I can't wait to get home and not eat!" She was born in England to Scottish parents and later moved to America, where she married.

Recently I visited a spiritualist church to watch a display of mediumship. As mentioned, I tend to couch my requests as "green lights." The medium singled me out and said, "A woman is coming to you; you knew her in childhood, old enough to be a grandmother but not so. She kept to the English ways, making Christmas pudding with coins in it, that sort of thing. She says, 'Go for it.' She is showing you a green light."

I felt bolstered and connected by this experience.

One Hundred Decades of the Rosary

Years ago, I was a social worker in the gritty areas of child protection and mental health. I had been craving a career change for some time.

I auditioned for a broadcasting course at a journalism college. When the letter finally arrived, I was disappointed to read I had missed out—by one place! Jon and I were due to head off to Africa, so I set myself a goal: I would recite one hundred decades of the Rosary over the course of our trip and then hand over the outcome, content I could do no more. (The Rosary is split into sets of ten Hail Marys, or decades, punctuated by other devotions. In all, I thought it involved around 1,400 prayers.)

Each day, as we relished our safari-on-a-shoestring, I was silently praying. Praying as we glimpsed our first giraffe in the distance. Praying as we settled in by a waterhole to watch the lions and elephants meander down. Praying at night as we washed dishes by the headlights of the truck.

When we got home almost two months later, a relative met us at the airport. The first thing she said? "You're in." I started the broadcasting course within weeks!

Of course, you don't need to dive into a marathon prayer session to receive signs and answers. A short, heartfelt petition is just as effective. I also realized, years later, that I got the spiritual math wrong and completed way more prayers than I needed to. Clearly, the Universe took pity on me and delivered that extra seat.

Niche Workshop

I present workshops around the concept of pre-birth soul plans, inspired by a seminal out-of-body experience of going to the Other Side. There, in the afterlife, I met the soul of a little boy. He was lovingly determined to send a message to his mother, whose deep grief blinded her to the signs he was sending. I was no more than a go-between.

Women struggle not only with their grief, but often deep guilt in the aftermath of a miscarriage or termination. Given this, I feel especially drawn to serve women who have endured pregnancy loss and neonatal death. And while I work one-on-one with clients, I had been thinking about designing a workshop tailored to women in these circumstances; I hoped they might offer each other support beyond the gathering. I was mulling this idea and asked out loud, "Am I supposed to be doing this work?" At that moment, my social media pinged. Up popped a specific question from a woman: *Does anyone know about souls who miscarry?*

It was another sign guiding me in the right direction, promptly answering my request.

Mr. Subagio, Translator Extraordinaire

Last spring, I was researching some immigration issues for a family member and needed a few documents translated from Indonesian to English. I had to send originals of a passport and birth certificate, so I was concerned they could land in the wrong hands. I called on the Other Side—and my father, who had passed—asking them to connect me with someone trustworthy.

There were only two people in the entire state accredited to do this particular translation, and one was around the corner from us. When I met Mr. Subagio, I was taken aback by how much he reminded me of Dad—both physically and temperamentally. His speech was so familiar, and he possessed the same quiet dignity. As I walked through his front door, having never met him, he reached out and cupped my face in his hands. It felt completely natural.

As I drove away, it occurred to me: Mr. Subagio lived on Young Street. *My last name.* How could I have not noticed that before?

We have remained in contact. I would have been grateful simply for a good translator; the Universe added the cherry on top with all the parallels to my father. I believe Dad connected us.

Others' Experiences

Guided to the Right House . . .

When my parents started to have trouble navigating the stairs, my sister and I knew we had to find a new home for them. Neither was ready for assisted living, but because of their advanced age, they couldn't travel to look at potential homes. My sister and her husband had recently identified Nashville, Tennessee, for their own retirement. Having always lived near my parents, my sister felt that moving them to Nashville would make the most sense.

I live in Asheville, North Carolina, and at the time my husband was quite ill with late-stage cancer. But I was closer to Nashville than my sister and parents in Baltimore, so it was decided I'd be the advance person to visit homes with a realtor.

On a steaming August day, we identified a potential home. Because of my husband's poor health, I had only one day to make a ten-hour round trip to Nashville. I would leave at 5:00 a.m., meet the realtor at 10:00 a.m., and make it home to my ailing husband before it got too late. He was home alone and also taking care of our dogs, so it was imperative I get back as soon as I could.

As I sat in the driveway of the house, I prayed that God and my angels would show me some signs so I would know if this was the right house for my parents. There were few homes in their price range, so if this one didn't work out, it would likely mean a long search for which I had no time. I knew that my mother and father, being independent people, were reluctant to make such a major purchase, sight unseen. But there wasn't really a choice. They had to trust me to make a decision—and I wasn't feeling confident.

When the realtor arrived, we entered via the back patio door. On the kitchen window was a large blue and white sticker that read "Proud Member of the U.S. Navy Reserve." My father was a proud career Navy veteran whose entire life revolved around his military service. And he was still a member of the Navy Reserve. I smiled.

We toured the rooms. Upstairs, I looked out a window to see a bird's nest. It was empty and had obviously been there for some time. My father loved birds. Just a few days earlier, he had asked me, "Will there be birds where we're going?" The nest answered his question in a way I never could have.

As I walked around the attic, I opened cupboards and cabinets. Lying inside on one of the shelves was a reproduction print of a painting of Jesus. The print, although unframed, was almost exactly like the framed print of Jesus that my father had kept over his dresser for my entire life.

After the realtor and I finished our walk-through, I called my parents to say I felt it was the "one," and I shared the signs. My sister was also on the call. Both she and I knew these signs were guideposts; we signed the contract that day. It all came together: I returned home to my ill husband on time. My parents had a home to move to within months. My father passed away a few years later, but my 94-year-old mother still lives there. The bird's nest sadly blew away last year, but the sticker remains on the kitchen window. The picture of Jesus stands in the cabinet for safekeeping and to remind my family of the signs.

—*Laura, Asheville*

. . . and to the Right Job

Life in Mumbai meant grueling commutes and twelve-hour days. My wife, Veathika, worked in the media, and it was near impossible to snatch waking hours together. We wanted out. My parents lived in New Delhi, and my in-laws were based in Dubai. We were enticed by this multicultural city in the Middle East with a good work-life balance and tax-free income.

Within weeks, Veathika was headhunted by a Hindi-focused radio station. A third of the population in Dubai is Indian (the largest expat community), so our culture held significance. I encouraged her to join her parents ahead of me.

When Veathika arrived, she printed one hundred copies of my résumé and handed them out to anyone who might help. Even if the connection to my industry (banking) seemed remote, she would thrust my résumé on them.

Seven months later, I visited Veathika for a week. I had only two weeks of annual vacation, so this was my sole chance to bag a position. Veathika went out of her way to line up interviews for me, but most people brushed her off with vague promises to keep my résumé on file. On my last day in Dubai—two hours before I was due at the airport—I got a call from Standard Chartered Bank, requesting a formal interview. I told them that I might miss my flight and wasn't appropriately dressed. The hiring manager laughed and said, "That's all right. Even if you're in your undies, I'll be happy to talk to you." We rushed over; the position was a perfect fit for my skills. The man who led the corporate sales team skipped the interview and wrote an offer on a piece of paper (which I still carry today). I was over the moon. I asked him how he had received my résumé; he simply shrugged and said he had been struggling to find someone with my experience. I'd never felt such euphoria—it was like winning the lottery! I couldn't sleep for three days. I joined the bank as an assistant manager and left twelve years later as the country manager for Governance and Risk across five countries in the Middle East.

I still don't know whom to thank for passing my résumé to the exact person who could offer me this golden opportunity. Whoever you are, I thank you profusely! Help can come from the most unexpected quarters. Uncanny.

—*Mehul Raina and Veathika Jain, Brisbane*
(via Mumbai and Dubai)

The Monroe Institute

I had heard about the concept of remote viewing from people who attended courses at the Monroe Institute in Virginia. At the time, however, the Monroe did not offer this particular course.

I was fascinated, but it was going to be expensive with airfares from Australia and accommodation—not to mention the cost of the course itself. I asked the Universe for not one, but *three* signs. One sign was not going to cut it with me!

The following week, I was pleasantly surprised to hear from a friend out of the blue; it had been months since we were in contact. He told me about a TV documentary on remote viewing that I should watch. I acknowledged to the Universe that I had one sign; I needed two more, or I wasn't going to budge.

A month or so later, my mum gave me a video as a birthday present. As it started to play, I saw a man I'd read about undertaking a remote viewing session. This man was married to a woman from the Monroe Institute. I knew this to be a sign, but reminded the Universe I would not go to the US unless I had three in total.

Two weeks later, I got a call from my friend Sarah, who asked if I had ever considered doing remote viewing. I had my three signs; I then flew to Texas for the remote viewing course. It was an amazing experience.

—*Sandy F., Perth*

The High Seas Beckon

Asking for signs and following my heart sparked a deeper self-love and love for my partner Brian, a professional sailor. It also led to an entirely new career. I am now an experienced first mate, chef, and chief steward who has traveled to Spain, the Red Sea, Ibiza, and the Canary Islands, to name a few.

At the time, my friends thought I was crazy, as I'd recently been nominated for the Telstra Women in Business Awards for my well-being center, Holistic Harmony. They assumed I was simply following Brian, but I am an energy healer and attuned to my gut feelings. Admittedly, I had built an extensive clientele around an approach that blended mainstream medicine, complementary medicine, and integrative medicine, but I honored my intuition.

Around this time, Brian's friend Frank (another yacht captain) was heading to France for work. Brian nominated us as a delivery crew. Two weeks later, Frank asked us to help him take a yacht from Cannes to the British Virgin Islands. The vessel was a 105-foot catamaran, and the job involved more than delivering the vessel; it was permanent work.

I resisted. I asked the Universe for a sign, and a couple of birds flew close by. I saw birds at my parents' windows when each transcended, so birds have long represented travel to me. That same day, a girlfriend announced she was moving to Spain and emailed me a photo of a sailing catamaran. The signs were staring me in the face.

I approached my staff to run the center, but they freaked out at the responsibility. It was disappointing, but I asked the Universe for guidance and went for a walk. The number 11 repeatedly showed up; it represents new beginnings. I also kept seeing "For Sale" signs. I felt a huge weight drop.

I sold my business. We bought a round-trip ticket and stopped off in the Bahamas to participate in the annual Antigua yacht races. While there, we were asked to deliver a 145-foot motor yacht to Genoa, Italy. We then got offered work on a brand-new French-designed sailing catamaran. We stayed in Europe for fifteen years, including time in Monaco and France.

—Beverley Holt, energy healer, podcast host, and co-author of Lady X, *Sydney*

A "Tree" Meditation

I was living in a country town five hours' drive from Adelaide, and my children were in secondary school. I had been thinking that I would need to move to the city in the next few years to manage their tertiary education needs. My aging parents also lived in Adelaide, and I wanted to be able to support them more.

I applied for a job in Adelaide, and one Friday morning I was offered an interview in the city the following Monday. I arranged my flights.

All that Friday and the next day I was quite unsure if I had made the right decision. I decided to do my "tree" exercise. On Sunday night before going to sleep, I meditated for fifteen minutes then nominated one arm as my "yes" arm and the other as the "no" arm, holding myself straight and tall with arms out, like a tree. I then asked, "Is this job the right one for me at this time?" I went to bed.

The following morning, I repeated the meditation, holding my body in the same posture, and asked the question again. Immediately my "no" arm felt heavy and dropped. I had my answer. I felt light and reassured. Spirit had led me to the right decision. I canceled the interview and have never regretted doing so, even though the job was a good one. It just wasn't the right one for me at that time.

—*Liz Hodgman, Adelaide*

Recurring Numbers

I teach manifestation workshops and practice energy healing. Often, the initials of my business (ZME) will appear again and again as license plates.

Numbers also speak to me. Many people take comfort in recurring sequences, say 444 or 555. With me, 108 crops up repeatedly. For example, I was catching a plane to visit a friend in Portland, Oregon, and I took Flight 108. She lived at number 108, and we used bus 108 to get around town.

—*Zoe Mac, energy healer, Burleigh Heads, Queensland*

An Auspicious License Plate

My build is petite and buxom. I was a shy teenager, and I didn't welcome the attention from boys. But as I got older, it took on a more serious issue with severe back and neck pain. I would research surgery on breast reductions for hours, only to chicken out. This went on for years. Finally, I decided I had to either do it or accept life as it was.

I was driving alone one night, still weighing the risks (it was elective surgery, after all) when a car cut in front of me. I was about to beep the driver—then gasped when I saw the license plate. It was DDxx x36C (I've crossed out the other details in case the plates are still in use). There it was: the DD cup size I currently was, and the 36C I hoped to be. Of course, I had the surgery, and I feel so much better.

—N., global citizen

Guided to a New Town

I had been traveling full-time for more than a year and was looking forward to being back in Australia.

I kept hearing the word "Burleigh" in my mind. Burleigh Heads is a coastal area in Queensland, and its beaches are known for great surfing. Sometime before in Germany, I'd had a reading by a medium in which the word came up. Now, it seemed to be popping up more frequently.

Eventually, I found myself in Burleigh, but the rental market was dire for tenants; some properties attracted as many as two hundred applicants. To make it more challenging, I was seeking a lease of only six months. I've long followed my intuition, staying in alignment. This always means that more signs appear.

I saw four potential rentals. One had an ocean view but was filthy. Another was unusually noisy. Eventually, I settled on one with big windows with both ocean views and hinterland views.

I was delighted to spot a whale from the balcony of that apartment and considered its appearance an affirmation and a sign.

—Zoe Mac, energy healer, Burleigh Heads, Queensland

Led to Courage

I work at a corporation with a less-than-stellar reputation for treating its staff well (especially interns). I was approached by a younger colleague for help with an issue she was battling. I gave her emotional support and secretly hoped that would be enough; I was up for promotion and didn't want to rock the boat ahead of the decision. But I couldn't shake the feeling I wasn't doing enough.

I began to ask myself: am I going to sit on the fence or make an effort? And that's when the giraffes showed up. Yep. Giraffes. I started seeing them in magazines. Then a TV commercial. One full-page ad jumped out, saying, "Stick your neck out." The final one (just to hit me over the head) was a friend who forwarded me a poster for sale, which featured a mother giraffe and her foal. I got the picture.

—Prisha, electrical engineer, Ankara

An Unexpected Job Offer

My mother used to work at a motel. Her boss had a Mercedes-Benz convertible, and she would take Mum for drives. Mum mentioned over the years how nice her boss was and that she would like a car like that one day. In Mum's later years, when we were looking after her, the comment kept playing on my mind. I wasn't consciously looking to purchase a car but was perusing online car auctions and came across a sporty Mercedes hatchback. I showed my husband, who called an associate from his previous job. This man had the vehicle assessed and bid on our behalf.

My husband had been out of the auto industry for a few years and enjoyed chatting with his old colleague. Around this time, his workplace was going through some challenging times. I could see the toll it was taking on him.

Shortly after, he called another old industry colleague who immediately asked, "You're not calling about the job, are you?" My husband replied, "No, just catching up." They talked about mutual interests and associates. Again, the man interrupted in a quizzical tone, asking if he was sure he wasn't calling about the vacancy. No, my husband assured him. The third time the man inquired, my husband said, "Tell me about the job."

Today, he's working at the business and enjoys it.

—Michelle, South Australia

Overheard Advice

I arrived in the city early ahead of a job interview for a radio voice-over position and ducked into a coffee shop to kill some time. As the line inched forward, I overheard two people in front of me. They were talking about hard-to-pronounce words, and one of them said, "Oh, yeah. Like when someone says something's gone 'awe-ree' instead of 'awe-rye' [awry]." I stopped; I'd always said it the first way, the way they were mocking. Think about someone who mispronounces a word. Maybe they say Brook-LINE, New York, or Bris-BANE, Queensland. You instantly know they're winging it.

Twenty minutes later, in my job interview, "awry" came up in the verbal test. Applicants were allowed only three errors. I felt like the Universe had nudged me to keep me in the game.

—Pisces, Sydney

Peacocks at a Retreat

We have a rural property in southern West Australia, and it had long been a dream of mine to run retreats for women here. I wanted the attendees to focus on reclaiming themselves, recognizing their inner beauty and gifts to the world.

It involved tremendous work. In the early stages, we used a nearby restaurant/function center, which gave us the chance to set up the space from scratch. This was a great opportunity for a recovering perfectionist to learn and stretch! I also co-facilitated some workshops with a friend.

On my first retreat, two peacocks arrived and stayed for hours. Their beauty, confidence, and presence—just as I was encouraging the attendees to acknowledge their own inner and outer beauty, and to stay present—was a powerful sign that I had been directed to manifest this retreat.

—Fin James, energy alignment mentor,
Denmark, Western Australia

Trusting My Intuition

I'm Australian but lived in California for fifteen years. During that time, I developed a personal meditation practice but didn't yet have a deeper understanding of its role in my life. Whenever I would meditate, I would feel an uncanny call back to Australia. I could see a quiet life with my Aussie family teaching yoga and meditation. This made little sense to me at the time, as I did not regard meditation as a viable career, and I loved my job in the US as a firefighter-paramedic.

After two to three years of these intuitions, I planned a trip back to Australia to explore what it would be like to live there. The trip left me wondering whether I would return to the US one final time simply to pack up my gear. I even researched shipping containers for moving my fifteen years' worth of belongings, but they were several thousand dollars each. I had great friends and had established a life stateside. Even though the stressful aspects of my job were beginning to take their toll, I couldn't imagine leaving it. This began an ongoing push-pull in my mind. Moving back to Australia felt too big and scary; I would flirt with the idea and then back away, overwhelmed.

Then, the Universe presented me a blessing disguised as disaster: a week before Christmas, my home burned down. As the shock registered and then began to subside, I saw with clarity what had happened. Firstly, the day it occurred, my dog was with me, not at home as usual. It could have all been so different. Secondly, I had been anxious about packing up all my things; now, I was free of that baggage—literally. Around the time I had moved to that house, I'd planned on canceling my renters' insurance, but the company had persuaded me to transfer the policy to my new address. The payout from the insurance meant I was both free of my possessions and had a lump sum to kick-start my next chapter. I took a six-month sabbatical to consider a complete career change. Could I really follow this bizarre intuition to teach meditation and yoga?

I returned to Australia and, still undecided, both trained to be a yoga teacher and applied for a paramedic job in Sydney. I was accepted straightaway to work as an Intensive Care Paramedic, attending the most stressful emergency calls. I had a foot in each camp, between the pace and stress of the ambulance, and the philosophy and practice of yoga; I could not have been straddling more divergent careers. At one point, I attended the scene of a car accident that was so distressing, it left me with a clenched jaw.

Around this time, I met a woman who had been on retreat in Hawaii. Listening to her describe her experience gave me goosebumps; I knew this was what I wanted to run myself. I continued to feel the push-pull of indecision. I would feel ready to make the change, only to step back from the brink. There was another factor to consider: I had signed a twelve-month lease on a rental in Sydney. As I got to know the neighbors, they warned me that my house was prone to flooding in torrential rain. I raised this with the property manager, who insisted all the issues had been addressed. Still, I got written confirmation that if the house ever flooded, I would be released immediately from my lease, with my security deposit returned in full.

A short time later—within five weeks—things developed in rapid fire in what I now affectionately call the "series of breakdowns."

My dog got cancer and needed surgery.

My car broke down, and it took more money than it was worth to fix it.

I had a breakdown at work and wanted to quit. They talked me into trying a new location with a quieter station and no night shifts.

I returned home that same night to discover that my fridge, like everything else in my life, had broken down. I laughed and cried at the irony. I could sense, inside, that the Universe was conspiring to force my hand in what I was too afraid to do.

Still, I resisted. I agreed to the new work arrangements. I packed my food into coolers, found a fridge online, and arranged with a friend to use his pickup truck to collect it the next day. That morning, he called to say he was too hungover to drive, and we rescheduled pickup for the following day. That very same night, amidst a raging storm, the house flooded. I woke up at 4:00 a.m. to the sound of my dog sloshing through water. I stood in the mess, doors flung open, and my arms raised to the howling sky.

The landlord let me out of the lease. A week later, I found myself on retreat in Sri Lanka. From that moment forward, I have never ignored the signs.

—*Kate Duncan, insight meditation teacher and yogi, Adelaide*

An Apparition of Mary Magdalene

Trusting my signs led me to become an Amazon #1 best-selling author of a collaborative book called *Lady X* in 2020. Mary Magdalene guided me to this.

The year before, I had asked for a sign for the next part of my journey. Soon after, a friend invited me to visit Mary Magdalene's grotto in Sainte-Baume, in the south of France, where she allegedly lived for thirty years. I quickly accepted.

The day after we arrived, we allowed plenty of time to experience the forest and walk the famous path of pilgrimage to her grotto. We climbed the mountainside for hours, slipping and sliding and getting lost. I asked for a sign. Despite our remote location, my phone buzzed shortly afterward, and the directions to the grotto came up on Google Maps. We had come close to the cave quite a few times, but it is concealed by a large boulder.

We saw a statuette of Mary Magdalene in a crevice and gasped as we turned: the cave entrance looked like a vagina. I ventured cautiously inside. We weren't prepared with flashlights, and the light from my phone was dim. But I wasn't afraid—despite my imagination running wild.

We went back outside and sat to meditate at the entrance. I asked Mary Magdalene to fill me with her divine love. Then, I asked her to help me have the courage and strength to make the best decisions for my soul's journey and to understand my life's purpose.

We sensed a change in temperature and immediately opened our eyes. Our hearts filled with divine love, joy, and contentment as we saw an apparition of Mary Magdalene. Initially, she appeared as a wispy white mist looking vaguely feminine. She evolved into a more solid shape: a tall, slender woman wearing a long white robe with a hood. Her hair was dark and wavy, flowing down to her waist. She seemed to grow taller, filling the entrance as she emanated a soft white light. The air felt deliciously fragrant and sweet.

She told me to keep helping women and to write a book on self-love. Soon afterward, I was asked to contribute two chapters to a book on that very topic. I wrote them on a sailing trip around Corsica with my friend Marie. We kept passing towers; I had read earlier that Magdalene is rooted in the Hebrew word "migdal," meaning tower. *Lady X* launched on 11/11/20 at 11:00 A.M.—a powerful spiritual day and equally powerful numbers. Whenever I see the number 11, I stop to breathe and ask my spirit guides to fill me with divine love.

In Australia I have found the most divine rose balm. Whenever I close my eyes to smell it, I see a vision of Mary Magdalene which warms my heart, and I ask for her guidance. Every time I'm considering a certain direction and ask if I'm on the right track, someone gives me a pink rose—even random strangers. This represents Mary Magdalene. I am looking for land to start an eco-village and school. With her guidance, I know I will find it.

I created a Mary Magdalene meditation. Many friends and clients tell me they receive amazing healings and experiences during it.

—Beverley Holt, energy healer, podcast host,
and co-author of Lady X, *Sydney*

CHAPTER THREE

Support

I t was a pang of envy so fleeting and yet I can recall it decades later. I was in college, and a friend was venting about another student who sounded like the roommate from hell. Many of us could relate, but her way of coping was much less common. "Oh well," she sighed. "If he's not out by the end of the month, I'll just have someone from my mom's law firm send him a letter."

If only we all had powerful backup at our fingertips. My family had no such network to tap. But while we may not have had an army of lawyers to draw on, we did have a phalanx of angelic soldiers and loved ones on the Other Side whom we could petition for help. My go-to in these situations is Archangel Michael, often depicted in warrior gear. We can summon him into battle for us at any time, under any circumstances, and he will charge in with his sword raised and colors flying.

My Experiences

The Scent of Rose Oil

I was working as a reporter-producer on a documentary. The executive producer was becoming a concern—not in a leery way, but more so for his unprofessional conduct—and I knew I had to call him out on his behavior. I didn't want a rushed conversation in the corridor, so I made a time to sit down with him.

The night before, with Jon out of town, I was chatting to God and sharing my concerns about the next day. Suddenly, I found myself speaking in a way that was oddly specific for me. Until then, my nighttime prayers resembled a laundry list of requests: please help this person, please help that one. This time I heard myself say, "I want two big angels to walk in with me to the meeting. I want them to stay, and I want them to leave with me."

Even as I said it, I almost laughed out loud; this was not the way I usually talked to the Universe. Still, something felt good about it (and feelings are the language of the soul).

The next day, the meeting went surprisingly well. I was calling out the man on quite pointed issues, yet he took it. Even he seemed surprised at the way we found common ground.

That night, I was talking to my angels, and I began to thank them. "I know you were there," I said. "Thank you." What happened next is seared into my heart. The room filled with the smell of rose oil. Not light, fragrant fresh flowers; this was heavy, aromatic, pungent rose oil. Logic intervened, and I padded around our apartment, looking for flowers I might have forgotten about. Of course, I found nothing. It was then that I relaxed and realized who it was.

All through the next day, I seemed to be floating. Nothing and no one could have bothered me or swayed me from a sense of being . . . centered.

It was the day after that when I sat down at my computer. I googled something like "rose oil + angels," and there it was: *For centuries, rose oil has signified the presence of angels.* As a journalist, it felt good to have my feelings corroborated by other sources. But at the same time, there was an inner knowing that surpassed any need for it.

A Bedside Figure

It had been an especially exhausting day. Jon was scheduled for outpatient surgery, and the hospital required us there at the crack of dawn. Add to that, we had recently made an offer on a house, and the agent was pushing things forward; I could not get her to hold off one day. The procedure went well, and I got Jon home and settled in bed. I was craving sleep, but a client had a rush job that couldn't wait. Instead of sinking into bed, I braced for several more hours in the study.

Finally, around 3:00 a.m., I eased open the bedroom door so as not to wake Jon. I had left on a bedside light, and what I saw took my breath away. There was a figure by Jon's side. It seemed feminine, young, and rather filmy in appearance. In one fluid motion, she seemed to "sit" by his bed and reach over like a loving parent to mop his brow.

I then realized I had been holding my glasses in my hand; the figure should have been a blur.

At that moment, I remembered I had visited the hospital chapel that morning after Jon was admitted, asking for help to get through the day. The figure did not acknowledge me in any way; I had been allowed to see her, and that was plenty. Her visit was a crucial reminder that we can ask for help, and it will be sent.

Jolted Awake

I was driving home one night after seeing my father in his nursing home, drained from making extra visits ahead of leaving town on an overseas trip. I contemplated pulling into a hospital parking lot to get some sleep, even though it was only a forty-minute drive home.

I seemed to get a second wind and believed I was okay to continue, though in retrospect, perhaps not as alert as I had first thought. I passed a train station, and I was startled to my core to see a frail, elderly man starting to cross the road. He was severely bent over, shuffling along alone at that time of night. It jolted me. I did a U-turn, wound down my window, and offered to take him home. He was lovely but declined. I gently insisted, as it didn't feel right. I assured him it was no trouble, adding that I was alone in the car (in case that made him feel safer). But he declined again and waved me off, so I felt I should respect that.

I turned back toward home and looked in my rearview mirror. The man was gone. There was simply no way, at his glacial pace, that he could have hobbled anywhere in the seconds it took me to turn around. I reasoned that he could have walked across the road and straight into a house.

Shortly after that, I was driving along the same stretch of road during the day, and realized with a shock that the man could not have walked into any house. The train station is opposite a former army barracks, and the premises are surrounded by a long barbed-wire fence!

I believe my angels jolted me awake to prevent an accident.

I didn't know it at the time, but my father would pass only weeks later. A friend suggested what I saw that night was my father's spirit, spending time between earthly and spiritual realms as he prepared to transition. When she said this, I had a visceral reaction. I was instantly covered in goosebumps and felt tears prick. I immediately remembered that the man's posture was identical to the way Dad would move when he used his walker. I believe that our souls leave our bodies more frequently as we prepare to transition to the Other Side. The man's age and vulnerability jolted me in a way a younger person would not have.

The Gratitude Journal

My sister-in-law Sharon was looking for a house, and she was concerned that because their own home had been snapped up, the clock was ticking to find a new property. We talked about asking for "the right house, at the right time, at the right price." She would keep her gratitude journal going, and I offered to do the same. Each night, we would reflect on the day, find things to be thankful for, and ask for the right home to show up.

That same afternoon, I received a parcel in the mail: a stylish gratitude journal from a close friend in Portland, Oregon.

It felt like a powerful sign of support. I had set an intent to be more mindful of gratitude, and the Universe delivered the favorite way I preferred to record these moments.

A Buddhist Meditation—on a Top 40 Station?

I had been getting by on little sleep as multiple project deadlines converged, and I was talking to Source while driving to the store. As I fiddled with the car radio, it played unusual music. I checked; it was tuned to our regular station. But this was nothing like its typical playlist—it sounded like a Buddhist meditation. I drove into the parking spot and stayed to listen. It was beautifully soothing. As I punched other stations, it resolutely stayed with the music, uninterrupted.

There was no logical explanation, but the meditation music was a clear sign to slow down.

Others' Experiences

Support Amid Heartache

I think loved ones visit when we're asleep. One day I was having a daytime nap. I was pregnant (about seventeen weeks), and I'd been having some spotting. I was worried, but the doctor wasn't. In my dream I was lying on my bed and woke (still dreaming) to see Mum standing next to me. I said, "Have you come to take my baby?" She didn't answer, but gave a little smile then bent down to kiss my cheek. *I actually felt it.* The next day I miscarried.

—*M., Perth*

Builders Come Out of the Woodwork

Our house plans have taken two years to nail down. Between the heritage council, the county, and various other stakeholders, it seemed to take forever. A spike in the local construction industry during COVID-19 made the whole process slower and more complicated. It seemed impossible to elicit a response, let alone a commitment, from any builders or even individual tradesmen.

One night, I was saying bedtime prayers with my eight-year-old, Flynn, and we moved through our list of family and friends. Then we asked for help with the builders for our new home. By the next morning, three different builders had emailed. That night, a relative phoned with the name of a fourth contact.

—*Holly, Perth*

Doormat on the Highway

Who says angels only help with the big stuff? We had a young and growing family and were renovating and extending our house; money was tight. Each time someone came bustling in through the back door, mud and dirt tracked in behind them. It drove me to distraction, trying to keep the floors clean, and I longed for a simple doormat.

We finally went shopping for one and couldn't believe how expensive they were; my husband refused to pay. We were driving home and turning off a major highway into our suburb, when in front of us—in the middle of the turn lane—lay a large doormat made of coconut husk. Exactly what we needed and had been shopping for! It must have dropped off a truck or trailer at the exact entry point into our neighborhood. We were astounded, but pulled over to the side. With some careful maneuvering, my husband dodged the cars and snagged the doormat!

—*Jennie, South Australia*

Angelic Help with Technical Reports

I worked at a National Laboratories campus, where my role involved a lot of technical report writing. While I was certainly competent at my job, I was overcome with writer's block whenever I sat down to compile our findings. The words that stared back at me on the paper were so subpar, I feared I would lose my job. This was not false modesty; I was genuinely panicked.

I began to pray fervently to Archangel Michael, imploring him to help me. I would pray for about fifteen minutes, and then out of the blue, words and phrases would start to pour out of me. They flowed so thick and fast, I would feel my hand cramping;

I could hardly keep up. This never happened at my keyboard, only when I put pen to paper. It was almost like a "channeling" or connection that you don't get with typing. The caliber of the submissions was simply beyond my level at that time.

I believe Archangel Michael saved my job.

—Annette Y., Santa Fe, New Mexico

Help at the Cash Register

My hometown welcomed a group of Afghan refugees in the aftermath of the Taliban taking control in August 2021. We were keen to help and joined a local clothing drive. I headed to a discount store and was delighted to find both adult and children's clothing for as little as one dollar. I scooped up T-shirts, pants, even pajamas. I returned a second time to stock up.

On my third trip, I filled a cart once more. As I waited in line at the register, I began to worry. I had already gone over budget; should I put some items back? I didn't want to, so I talked silently to Spirit. I asked it to keep an eye on the total and to let me know it was nearby.

The bill came to $123.45. Not only was it far less than I had expected, I can only imagine the odds of the numbers being in sequence.

I knew the angels had my back.

—Aquarius, Adelaide

Numbers Appear in a Dream

For a short while in the 1980s I was between jobs, and my resources were stretched thin. Meanwhile, I had two children in private school, and the bills arrived like clockwork.

My mother used to enjoy a little bet at the horse races twice a month. One night she had a dream that her favorite numbers came up. She saw the numbers appear on a wall, and they were so vivid, she woke up immediately. My father was an accountant and very logical; he dismissed her dream with a smile.

But Mum had a strong feeling. She asked me to place a fifty-cent bet for her. I matched that with another fifty cents, plus twenty-five cents each for my brother and sister.

Those numbers came through—our modest $1.50 sparked an $18,000 windfall! With my share, I was able to pay the school fees, buy the children new mattresses, and clear my car loan.

While the win itself was amazing, and such a gift from the Universe, it also showed me the power of recognizing and listening to signs. First, Mum had followed her intuition; a different person might have rejected it. By extension, I also chose to take a chance on her experience and stay open to the possibility that the numbers were a sign.

—*Sandy F., Perth*

Reunited with a Childhood Friend

After my marriage broke down, I moved with my three children to a rental for a year. I then decided it was time to stop paying off someone else's mortgage and buy my own home.

I eventually found a small place in an area called Maslin Beach. It was much more modest than our previous home, but I was drawn to it. Two things caught my eye: the pine trees that engulfed the front yard, and a shiny-leafed plant that had taken over a corner of the backyard. Both were reminiscent of my birthplace, a town called Millicent. I bought the house; it was something I did without having to depend on anyone else.

I only knew my neighbors with an occasional wave. Sharlene was around my age (late thirties) and lived across the road. She worked at our local fruit and veg shop, where I often did my shopping. We exchanged greetings, but nothing of a personal nature. One day I noticed she was absent and heard she was on vacation.

When she returned, I asked her about her getaway. She had visited Millicent to see her mum and her friends. You could have knocked me over with a feather—we had both been born there! We chatted a bit, but I had to leave, as I felt emotional and didn't want to make a fool of myself by crying.

Later that day, Sharlene rang her mum to tell her about me. Unbeknown to us, we shared a lot of history. Our mothers had been best friends! Sharlene and I had been close when we were little. She even showed me a photo of us as girls on her fridge; she had often wondered about her playmate. It was me. My family had moved after my mother passed away when I was four years old.

My memory was hazy, but she remembered quite a bit about us playing together. Years later, I found out why I liked a certain song by The Seekers called "Lemon Tree," and why I used to eat the gum off trees but never knew why. Sharlene is indigenous and had taught me about the gum, as her grandfather had taught her.

We had grown up in the same town, and where did I move in the aftermath of my marriage breakdown? To Maslin Beach, 260 miles away. Across the road from Sharlene.

When I look back, I see that my angels nudged me to a house and community across the state. This would guarantee that I met a childhood friend at a time and place I knew no one.

I soon visited Sharlene's mother, who shared many stories of my childhood.

Support for the future. A link to the past. Incredible.

—*Kerry Toth, writer and tarot card teacher, Adelaide*

A Voice, a Visit

I was twenty-six that summer and six weeks' pregnant with my fourth child when I had an unforgettable experience.

I was resting when I heard a voice tell me softly, "You won't experience the motherhood of this baby." It was a strong male voice, yet so gentle. I rubbed my tummy and could not imagine anything happening. I felt an overwhelming sense of peace.

About six months later, I had the exact same experience with the voice. I went full term, and the doctor induced labor. I somehow knew I would not be keeping this baby, but I held such strong hope. After an agonizing fifteen hours, my baby girl was born without a skull. I named her Barbara Joy Grace.

My husband at the time left me in my grief to go to a football game, where he got drunk. I was alone, devastated, and distressed. Amid this deep heartache, I felt the presence of my grandfather Tom, who had recently passed. He was such a kind soul, and we had enjoyed a special connection. I was overcome with the strongest feeling that Barbie was with him.

The next day my aunt came to get me—and inexplicably, she insisted on taking me to a department store. It was bizarre, but I didn't have the strength to resist. There, I encountered two people I believe were angels. In the bedding department, I saw a young woman with Down syndrome. She paused to look at me with utter love and compassion . . . and a certain knowing. I sensed acutely that she knew what I had gone through. This experience was overwhelming and took my breath away. We then walked around to the furniture section, and again there was another woman with Down syndrome. She, too, made a special connection. Nothing was said on either occasion, yet I was overcome with waves of love and support in a such a dark time. Their presence, and their effect on me, was no coincidence.

—*Chris, Perth*

Tapping Expertise on the Other Side

I believe that souls take their accumulated insights and education (formal or informal) when they return to the Other Side. There, they possess a powerful combination of all earthly knowledge and an unparalleled desire to help us. If you have a loved one on the Other Side who was known for a particular talent, you can call on them when you need their skills, just as you would have done here on earth. And while you're at it, why not shoot for the top? If a legal challenge is keeping you up at night, you can seek the counsel of a former Supreme Court Justice. Spiritual author Lorna Byrne suggests we call on "teacher angels" to help us learn something new. It's not about worshipping them or praying to them per se (although in essence, a prayer is simply a request or petition).

My understanding of tapping expertise on the Other Side has been broadened through meeting Nathan Castle. Nathan is both a medium and a Catholic priest (a combination that must have ensured some entertaining holiday dinners!). He has a fascinating principal clientele: souls who are stuck between realms.

Here, Nathan shares how he calls on souls on the Other Side to help him day to day—and how you can, too, just as easily. If talk of saints is something you're unfamiliar with, simply remember they are souls like us.

Help with Home Repairs

My grandmother lived next door and would walk around the house talking to Saint Anthony of Padua. When she was around sixty-five years old, she bought some do-it-yourself books about electricity and plumbing. She asked Saint Joseph the carpenter to help her rewire the house and build a bathroom in the garage. What's so strange about that?

When I talked to the saints, I usually sent a message up to heaven. But I knew that they could be here on earth too, like the day Mary showed up.

I was in the second grade when our church had a crowning ceremony in May honoring Mary. Her life-size statue was placed on an altar, flanked by lots of candles and flowers and steps leading up to it. Other kids had speaking parts. I wasn't picked, and I had to sit in the pew and sing a hymn; I was grumpy.

Then Mary showed up. I could see her inside me and hear her. She asked, "May I sit by you?" I nodded on the outside, but on the inside, I said, "We're not supposed to talk in church." So, there I was, correcting Mary, the Mother of God, about her behavior in a church named for her. That's how it began.

Many years later, I was a priest and pastor of a church named for Saint Andrew the Apostle. I felt overwhelmed and was advised to speak to him each morning about that day's work. I did that faithfully. On a particularly bad day he showed up to me. He didn't say anything, but he didn't need to. I got the message: he had my back.

Now when I need to write, I ask for writing saints. When I need to do computer tasks, I ask for geeky saints. There's always somebody who knows how to connect the wires to the cable box or figure out some other digital conundrum. When I wanted to get better at golf, I got a soul called Duffy. He invited along his dad, Archie. They're from Scotland, the birthplace of golf; Saint Andrew is its patron. When I'm feeling sad, there are joyful saints like Dominic. Heaven is full of happy souls. Just having them around changes my mood.

Sometimes I ask for famous saints, but not always. I ask them to come and help with stuff all the time. Other times, I ask for my grandmother who rewired her house and built a bathroom in her garage with Saint Joseph's help. What's so strange about that?

—Nathan Castle, OP*, author of
And Toto Too: The Wizard of Oz™ as a Spiritual Adventure
and the Afterlife Interrupted *series, Tucson*

*OP denotes Nathan's religious order of Dominican priests.

CHAPTER FOUR

Reassurance

S ometimes we simply want to know that everything will turn out all right; it makes all the difference in weathering a storm. Whether at home, at work, or in our community, we can get so caught up in a new development or challenge that we seek to be comforted as we work our way through it. Far from being a sign of insecurity, craving reassurance is a natural human desire.

And when that comfort comes, it's deeply affirming. When it seems elusive, we have a choice. We can give the situation more time, or we can hand over the outcome to the Universe. The power of surrender can play a critical role in our plans. Sure, "surrender" commonly means to give up a fight, but it applies far beyond defeatist terms. Just as it is a strength, not a weakness, to speak up when we need help, surrender allows a release in which we feel a weight lifted. We set aside resistance and open ourselves to new possibilities.

As adults, we like to call the shots; after all, hasn't every child longed to be a grown-up, tired of being told what to do and how to do it? We want to be masters of our futures. I believe that our otherworldly helpers understand how much we like to control our lives as adults—so when we hand over our worries, the Universe honors that.

To lose control of a situation can be disheartening enough; to consciously cede that control is a chance for genuine spiritual growth. Rather than dictating how a situation should be resolved or healed, we are simply staying open to how the Universe might deliver. This is not received passively; in fact, I believe that the act of surrender sparks tremendous angelic activity on the Other Side.

My Experiences

Our Future Shows Up—in an Old Newspaper

Though we tend to ask for signs to play out in our present or near future, it can be equally comforting to see them in hindsight.

Jon and I have kept a newspaper issued on the day we married. Like clockwork, it comes out whenever we move house. We always stop amid the packing paper and cardboard boxes to make coffee and spend a few minutes laughing at the hairstyles and the fashion. And it was all so cheap!

We had returned to Australia after sixteen years abroad. The plan was to move into a rental (on Kathleen Street) before settling into our home (on Elizabeth Street). This time when the paper came out, we ventured into the property section and noticed something that had escaped us in previous years.

There in the property listings were our transitional house on Kathleen Street and, in the next column over, *our own home* on Elizabeth Street. It was astonishing to see, decades prior, the web being spun for our plans. I felt reminded that a bigger picture was unfolding, and even though we could glimpse only small parts at a time, all would be well.

At this literal moment of transition, it was deeply reassuring. The Universe was lovingly conspiring to keep an eye on things.

From Tiny Ad to Feature Article

Settling in a new city takes enormous reserves of energy, with many moving parts. A dose of encouragement can make all the difference.

Jon and I had recently transferred to South Australia, and I was working to spread the word on my work around soul plans. At the time, I ran a small ad in the Saturday paper, as well as on social media. I submitted questions for a column that profiled people across the state. While my contact at the paper was gracious, he offered no guarantees; my name would be thrown in the mix along with many others over the next twelve months.

One Friday, I made a mental note to renew my little ad, but time escaped me. I was annoyed with myself for missing the deadline, because that Saturday fell on a holiday weekend, when people have more time to read the paper. On the train home, I talked to my angels about it and handed it over to them. "I've messed up," I said. "Please do whatever you can. I'm handing it over to you."

Early next morning, I headed out to meet friends when my phone began ringing nonstop. The first caller was Jon; he'd almost dropped his coffee when he had opened the paper to see my photo staring back, with an extensive article next to it. It was the column feature.

It dawned on me: I had missed the chance for a small paid ad, but the Universe delivered instead a feature piece, many times the column space. It was a sign of support that boosted me.

The IVF Nurse

I've never known firsthand the heartache of infertility, nor the grit and grace it demands. I have twice been an egg donor, though, and have witnessed these qualities in the two friends to whom I donated. IVF (in vitro fertilization) involves tremendous physical, emotional, and financial resources. And despite all this, the outcome is still a gamble.

In one instance, we received a powerful sign that all would work out well—and the stakes could not have been higher. I was having my eggs harvested (to then be fertilized in the lab), which involved general anesthesia. "Going under" is an altered state between life and death, and it was in this in-between state that I received a powerful sign. I met a sweet, plump old lady who stood by my side. She was calm and reassuring as she held my hand. She smiled so lovingly as she explained that a little boy was on his way.

When I woke up in the recovery unit, my friend Kate (my egg recipient) was waiting for me. I asked the attending nurse to find her older colleague so that I could thank her; her presence had made such a difference. The nurse seemed confused and insisted no one by that description had been present. I remembered the lady's name and shared it confidently. At this point, Kate blanched; it was an unusual family nickname for her grandmother, who had passed away years before. In time, Kate and her husband welcomed a baby boy.

A Sign Leaves Me Speechless

I found myself in need of an interior designer for *Divinely Align Me* at short notice. This unfolded around the holidays, when many people would be unavailable even to provide a quote, much less to make room for me in their calendars. We were due to start typesetting the pages within weeks.

At the time, I was reading a delightful book by Phil Bolsta called *Sixty Seconds: One Moment Changes Everything.* It's about seminal moments in the lives of forty-five people, including musicians, NBA stars, and leading spiritual authors such as Deepak Chopra and Carolyn Myss. I was pleasantly surprised to see mention of Saint Teresa of Ávila; it wasn't a religious title. I had a book about her in childhood, and I couldn't recall when I stopped calling on her help. I sent up a quick "hello" to heaven to say I'd be in touch more often.

That night, I spoke with my angels about my concerns around finding a designer. I asked them to show me what to do and to please make it quick; I was on a deadline.

The next morning, I recalled a recommendation about a year before. My trusted editor had suggested a colleague I should contact, but it had slipped my mind to follow up. What was her name, and would she even be available?

I found the email: her name was Tessa Avila. Could that be any closer to Saint Teresa of Ávila? And of course, Tessa is often short for Teresa.

At that point, I had no idea of Tessa's interest or availability. But this synchronicity hit me between the eyes, and for a moment I was speechless. I knew that whatever transpired, the Universe was there to support me.

Tessa graciously squeezed me into her roster, and her work has blended whimsy and substance.

Oh, and a final note on Saint Teresa. She was considered a great mystic. Who better to help me on a metaphysical book?

Others' Experiences

Shooting Stars and Jet Airplanes

In the months just before my husband passed away from cancer, I'd often step outside at night to walk our dogs before bed. I'd look up and ask God to send me a sign I wasn't alone. I'm not a person who often sees shooting stars, but in those early winter months of November and December when the trees were bare, whenever I asked for a sign, I often saw them. Sometimes they had remarkably long tails, so the vision lasted for what seemed like an extra-long time. If it wasn't a shooting star, I'd always—and I mean *always*—see a jet plane flying high overhead with its signal lights blinking in the night sky. My husband worked for the Federal Aviation Administration his whole career, so seeing airplanes was just as much a sign as a shooting star. God was telling me I'd be all right no matter the sadness I was feeling. I wasn't alone and never would be. For about a year after my husband died, I'd often see shooting stars, but not so much anymore. But every night—even now, seven years later—whenever I step outside and ask for a sign, there's always a jet passing overhead.

—*Laura, Asheville*

The Writing on the Bathtub

My husband and I were studying at the University of Maryland and living on campus in a small two-bedroom apartment with a private bathroom. We were both on full scholarships and barely saw each other then, as we raced between classes and home. He was a night owl and slept later.

I had been wondering for a while whether God existed (my husband was a staunch atheist). I decided to pray hard for seven straight days, after which I felt confident I would receive a sign. On the seventh morning, I went to shower ahead of a busy day. As I stepped into the bathtub, I looked down to see a black thread in one corner. When I peered closer, it was arranged to read the word "God" in perfect cursive writing; it even had an upper-case G. I stared, astonished at what I saw.

We were so poor then that all my clothes used to fit in one wash load, and none of them were black. My towel was green. I couldn't wait to show my husband, but he wouldn't be up for hours, and I had to get to class. I showered, careful not to disrupt the writing and the thread. I was certain this would convince him. But he must have showered without noticing it, and the shower water mangled the thread.

I was disappointed, but the sign had been for *me*.

—*Annette Y., Santa Fe, New Mexico*

The Birthday Card That Wasn't

I had been struggling with a series of challenges, and no matter how I tried, dark thoughts burrowed their way into my mind. I have had depression once or twice before in my life, and I felt this was going to be worse. I was running errands, and as I collected the mail, I spotted my aunt's handwriting. Inside was a card that read on the front: *God made you on purpose. For a purpose.* It was filled with encouraging words. The funny thing was, my birthday was a month before, and it wasn't in any way a birthday greeting. I believe my aunt was lovingly directed to choose that card and, just as significantly, to send it late, as it arrived in perfect timing to ward off the despair. I am forever grateful.

—*Manon-Camille, Paris*

The UN of Michaels

I was going through my second divorce and returning to night school. It seemed I was running from one thing to the other, and no matter how many things I checked off, more appeared.

My grandma used to speak about Saint Michael the Archangel when I was growing up. I had liked his battle gear, and stories about him had made Sunday School easier to bear.

Just when I didn't think I could take any more on my plate, my boss told me I was headed to an international conference. Normally, I would have jumped at the chance, but I felt the vein on my neck start to throb. My kids know that's a sure sign that Dad is going to lose it, but I kept calm.

Sure enough, I found myself on a plane, staring out at the clouds, when my grandma popped into my head again. Remembering Saint Michael, I said silently, *Hey, I could use some help. Show me that you're around and that you've got my back.*

The conference went for three full days, and I couldn't believe the people I was meeting. There was Mick from Australia at the opening night mixer, Michael from England at the first dinner, and then a Miguel from the US who sat next to me at a lecture. A Mikey helped me secure a ticket to a sold-out talk by a celebrity speaker. I had been doing a group activity with a guy called Henri, and later over drinks, I was telling him about all the Michaels and having a laugh (I kept the angel part to myself). I told him he'd broken the chain.

"Not so fast," he said over his wine. "Actually, I use my middle name. I was christened Michele Henri (Michael Henry)."

I had just been knocked over the head by the United Nations of Michaels.

—Bevan, Tokyo (via Chicago)

Birds and Feathers

When I first became an energy healer, extraordinarily powerful signs, especially birds and feathers, began appearing in my life. I was facing lots of fears stepping out into my new healing practice, and I remember a flock of blackbirds came to our house and stayed for the first few months through a big transition. One day, I was feeling concerned about an upcoming event I was hosting. Suddenly, an enormous blackbird flew into the French door next to me! It was the loudest bang ever, and it literally shocked me out of my negative thoughts!

In the days ahead, swirling circles of feathers would gather outside my French doors. More recently, I renovated my front entry, which according to feng shui should be "clear" and bright. I released all worries during the renovation, unconcerned about how long it would take, and I went with the flow. I really enjoyed it, and the day after we finished, cash blew onto my front lawn, right near my home office wall! It was amazing.

—Leigh White, transformational coach and
master quantum energy healer, Sydney

Penny from Heaven

My son and my ex-husband had a fractious relationship. It pained me to see them in conflict with their on-again/off-again dynamic. My son would say, "I hate Dad." Unfortunately, circumstances at the time meant that when my ex-husband died, we didn't learn about his passing until two weeks later. My son had no resolution.

One night soon after the news, he was pulling into the driveway and got out to move the gate. His friend was on the other side of the car. Suddenly, he felt a rush of air as something fell past his right side. It was a penny. Given the speed and force with which the coin hit the ground, it had to have been dropped from a considerable height. There was no logical explanation. The penny was the year 1945. In numerology, the numbers fold down to a single digit, which in this case is a perfect number 1 and spiritually significant. My son called me straight away. And then it hit us both: his father always used to say, "The penny has finally dropped." And it had. Literally. His father was telling my son all was okay between them. (Incidentally, the penny had fallen to his right side. When Spirit speaks to me, it's always in my right ear.)

—*Tricia Lock, Adelaide*

Dragonfly

One of the most significant instances that I've encountered was shortly after my position was made redundant at my old place of employment. A girlfriend and I were sitting on the bench outside our building on Hay Street (in Perth) as we often did, reflecting about all the fun times and laughs we had shared . . . when a dragonfly landed on my bag!

I was gobsmacked as I had never seen one before in the city. My friend told me it was my dad coming to say that it would all be okay. Well, it certainly was. Shortly after that, I was offered another position with my present employer.

The experience always stuck with me, and I had the warmest feeling the day the dragonfly chose to land on my bag. He stayed for a while and was quite comfy. He felt safe.

—*Colleen Guidetti, Perth*

Owls Bring Hope

My son was unemployed, and I was worried for him. I could see that the job search was taking a toll. I went into meditation to ask the Universe for a sign of support, and received a picture of an owl.

A few weeks later, I left for a long-planned vacation to the US. I was taking in a few states and would be staying with friends in Austin, Texas, for one part. This was not their home, but a holiday rental (they lived in Houston). As I walked into this somewhat random house, I saw art above the mantelpiece: it was a picture of three owls! I felt a peace wash over me; it gave me hope that everything would be okay.

By the time I returned home, my son had a new job.

—*Sandy F., Perth*

ALICIA'S NOTE: Sometimes signs come through other people and at other times through dreams. This next experience combines both. ∎

A Dream, A Staircase

An old friend had a son who was single. One night, I dreamed that we were at a beautiful and elegant celebration: champagne flowed, and the food was delicious. Everyone was in high spirits, and I asked my friend the occasion. "Oh, it's Arun's engagement party," she said.

I then looked up to see her son coming down a staircase, beaming with happiness.

I shared this dream with my friend, and it made her smile.

Over the next six months, unbeknown to me, my friend and her husband corresponded with another couple about their adult children. The families are from Sri Lanka, where arranged marriages are customary. Each party's astrological charts were drawn up, examined, and found to be a good match. However, both sets of parents were happy to have an intermediary make an introduction and to leave it at that; it would be up to their children if they felt a connection.

Arun and Adita spoke for nine months over the internet getting to know each other. He was based in Perth, and she in Adelaide.

At one point, Arun came to visit, and Adita met him at the airport. She found a discreet place to angle her mobile phone; it would capture the moment they met in person.

Just like the dream, the phone video shows Arun coming down a staircase (in this case, an escalator), and just like the dream, he was beaming with happiness.

—*Lourdie, Koondoola, Western Australia*

CHAPTER FIVE

Acceptance and Moving On

*I*magine for a moment that you're a baby again. You're cherished, coddled, and played with—everyone delights in you. "Life is good," you think, rolling around in your crib. "I'm going to stay this way forever." Except, of course, you can't. Because you are hardwired physically, emotionally, spiritually, and intellectually to progress and mature on every level.

Here, signs can help: They can unveil insights and circumstances that bring us to a point of moving on, breathing into a new space, even though we feel hesitant.

Have you ever felt you've outgrown a friendship? An old saying maintains that friendships exist based on mutual need. Maybe you met on the first day of middle school, when you were feeling vulnerable. Perhaps your children brought you together. Or you were interns at the same time. Then one person begins to stretch in a different direction, and connections start to fray.

Moving on—from a relationship, a job, or an old habit— takes courage. And the process is often gradual, incremental. During this transition, you must leave behind a way of being: a long-engrained way of looking at the world and your place in it. Even when the need is clear, it doesn't mean that moving on is easy. Other times, disappointment can soften into acceptance that people or situations may not change or evolve in our favor; all we can do is change how we react to them and how we let them play a role in our story. Signs can help point the way to a decision that gets us unstuck while providing encouragement along the way.

⟲
My Experiences

The (Other) City of Angels

I smile to think that my love of rom-coms helped me see a sign. We were living in the San Francisco Bay Area, and I was on the subway, silently talking to my angels. I felt stuck on the work front, planting seeds that seemed destined to wilt in a highly competitive market. I wanted to let go, but a good journalist is tenacious, right? I felt torn, trapped in a dilemma as to how much longer to pursue a particular position.

I asked for a sign that my guides were nearby and that all would be okay. Still lost in thought, I headed out of the subway and into the San Francisco Public Library for the first time. As I walked in, I paused to look up at the floors above, which were arranged in a circular structure. It seemed remarkably familiar, but I hadn't been there before.

I asked a librarian if there was ever a movie or TV show shot on location. Yes, she said, *City of Angels* with Nicholas Cage and Meg Ryan had been filmed in part at the library. It has multiple scenes showing people reading and studying, with their guardians by their side, and a pivotal shot where all the angels gather around the perimeter. Check it out.

I felt supported and heard. I could release the dogged mindset and expectations around this situation, knowing I would be supported in whatever came next. I had been holding myself in place, like a lab specimen suspended in formaldehyde. I was ready to free myself.

A Voice in the Shower

We were living in Chile, and my fortieth birthday was approaching. I was touched when close friends announced they would be flying in to celebrate with us. I'll always be grateful, as they did so at considerable cost and effort. We enjoyed sightseeing and took in the delights of this gorgeous South American country.

Still, something seemed amiss, and I struggled to define it. One day, the dynamic came into clear focus. I was loved by these women, and we shared deep history. But the bond between the two of them was hermetically sealed. I felt on the outside, and always would be. It was completely unintentional, and no one's fault; it was simply the way it was.

I was in the shower when the tears started to flow. I was lost in thought when I was startled by a voice outside myself, so deeply loving and calm. "Don't worry," it said soothingly. "They often come together." It was barely a handful of words, yet they were drenched in compassion.

I never mentioned this to my friends until I began to write this book; I hadn't wanted them to feel bad. I still don't. Today, I believe they are part of the same soul group, choosing to arrive together and adopting roles within a family or at least a shared community, where they were assured of forging strong bonds.

I believe I heard the voice of an angel that day to make me feel less alone in that moment. The support was dramatic and memorable, and it didn't end there. It ushered in a shift by managing my expectations moving forward. And that was a good thing.

Others' Experiences

"Leave Your Mother to Me"

I am Indonesian and married an Australian girl. We were living in Jakarta for many years when her parents asked us to return. My sister-in-law suffered MS and needed more care than they could provide alone. I wanted to help, but felt torn as my mother was elderly and ill.

I asked God for a sign as to what to do. Shortly after, my wife and I were traveling to a work site that I needed to check on. We were in the car when God spoke to me in my right ear. In Javanese English, I heard, "Leave your mother to me." I had my answer.

We moved to Australia, and my mother recovered to live many more years.

—Bapak Tomik Subagio, Adelaide (via Jakarta)

Elizabeth Gilbert's Petition

Moving on from a relationship demands its own blend of strength in the present and hope for the future. Even when the need to part ways is clear, we may need to call on reserves of courage we might never have known we had. Amid the dark times, we can still find moments of joyful release.

In her international best seller, *Eat, Pray, Love,* Elizabeth Gilbert recounts a wonderful moment of surrender to the Universe. She is at the end of her tether because of delays in her husband signing their divorce papers. On a road trip with a girlfriend, she decides to "petition" God to bring closure to this chapter. Not only does she sign the petition (metaphorically), but she joyfully adds more and more "signatories." Abraham Lincoln! Nelson Mandela! Mother Teresa! And Martin Scorsese, for good measure. You can feel the joy as she continues to add names to her list of supporters. She dozes off, her friend at the wheel. Soon after, Gilbert's lawyer calls: her husband had signed the papers.

I admire how Gilbert took control in asking for support, imploring the Other Side to help in any way it could. She wasn't aggressive in her demands but playful, having fun as she added more and more absurd signatories. In writing a symbolic petition, she gained clarity around her desires to move on.

I also love that while she made her wishes clear, she surrendered the outcome at the same time. She left it up to the Universe as to how circumstances would play out—and in doing so, drew support from myriad and unexpected quarters. She removed herself from emotional, financial, and legal limbo.

We can, too. We can harness the power of surrender.

A Startling Sign among the Junk Mail

I received a sign that forever changed how I interacted with my younger sister, Hannah. But first, you need to know that my name is Don and my last name starts with "D-o-i-t-h."

I had always struggled to say no to Hannah. Our mother died before my sister started school; I was a teenager. Hannah's memories of Mom were few and blurry by comparison. I harbored guilt that I had Mom much longer.

As she grew up, Hannah leveraged my guilt to ensure I helped her financially with a car, then an apartment. When she wanted a lump sum toward a home deposit, I helped her, even though it strained my marriage. I knew I had to set boundaries and say no.

The final straw was when Hannah demanded I arrange a credit card for her. Still, I struggled to release myself from this unhealthy dynamic—even when it sparked a bitter argument with my wife. Even when she pointed out (rightfully) that our own children had gone without things to help my sister. Even when she threatened to walk out.

Then the Universe sent a wake-up call that rattled me.

One night in the middle of all this, I headed out to clear our post box and maybe clear my head. Among the junk mail were several offers from credit card companies. I sifted through them with a wry smile and a made a mental note to shred the pile at home.

I threw the mail in my study and went to bed.

The next day, I picked up the junk mail and turned to the shredder. I noticed something that had escaped me the night before. A company had misspelled my name, and it formed a message I couldn't ignore. My middle initial was pushed together with my first name. Instead of reading "Don T. Doith____," it read "DonT. Doith____."

All I saw was: Don't Do It.

And of all the correspondence it could have appeared on, it was a letter from a credit card company.

I finally found the courage to move on from rescuing Hannah.

—*Don D., South Central Chicago*

Life-Changing Support at a Breaking Point

An experience at a critical stage in my life helped me walk away from a situation that was propelling me into darkness.

About ten years ago, I was going through an extremely stressful time with our family business. I was also battling chronic back and neck pain. I remember going to bed one night thinking that I would not wake up. Not that I was thinking of harming myself;

I was simply in so much pain and stress that I believed my heart would stop. I've since learned that this is referred to as "the dark night of the soul."

My hubby was an army officer and away from home all the time, so I was raising our daughters and running a failing family business by myself. My worries were overwhelming me: *Who would look after my girls? What will happen to Mum and Dad if the business fails?* I lay in bed, my head bursting from all my anxiety and tension.

Then I sensed that someone had knelt on the bed beside me. I thought maybe the dog had snuck into my room, but no. I felt it again on the other side of me, and then it seemed like someone was supporting my head. I was gently lifted from the bed, *cradled by three presences,* as all my pain was slowly released. I felt so safe. I knew that I was literally "in good hands" and that somehow, I would be okay. I would get through this ordeal and be stronger for it. After an hour or so, they gently laid me back on the bed. I slept a peaceful, restorative sleep—something that I hadn't been able to do for a long time.

I had always been spiritual, but this set me on an incredible path. Amazing people came into my life quickly after that night. With their wisdom and support, I was able to dramatically turn things around. I tapped an inner strength I didn't know I had, and was able to make hard decisions about the business and to walk away guilt-free. I even found a talented lady who helped me with my back issues. It was a truly life-changing experience.

—*Tammy N., Bruthen, Victoria*

Gambling on an Invention

I'm an inventor, and lately I've come to think that inventing can be an addiction, like gambling. You're always hoping the next device, gadget, or tweak will be the one where your ship comes in. I flew from Amsterdam to London for a meeting I was sure would change my life. All the prior talks and correspondence had gone well, yet when I got there, things were "off." For reasons I still don't fully understand, negotiations crumbled, and I lost the deal.

That night I was in my hotel room, full of despair. Despondency had taken root before, but I had always managed to shake it off. This time, the emotions stuck: anger, shame, failure.

I saw nothing, and I heard nothing. But the room changed. The air was different, as if charged with an otherworldly current. I felt deeply loved and supported. *I was enough.*

I wish I could say that things made a U-turn after that, that the other party saw the error of their ways and begged me to come back to the table. They didn't, but in that moment that "something" meant everything. I was shown a different way of being, and the whole team was there for me.

This marked a shift in my life. I was able to give my best to my inventions and ideas, but I could release the old expectations of how things should be: my way, my time frame, my process. I had been trapped in a certain mindset, and this freed me to consider other possibilities.

—*Dougal McS., inventor and designer, Amsterdam*

A New Direction

In India, there is a lot of fear around cockroaches. Beyond simply being a household pest, they are considered creatures of darkness, emerging as they do from crevices. That said, they rarely bite—so I was startled to find myself bitten twice in one day, just hours apart. What were the odds?

At the time, I was in my own period of darkness. I felt stuck, unable to move forward in my professional work. At its core was a fear of not being good enough. The cockroach bites made me reflect, and I knew I had to move forward. I leaped into action, starting with my home. I began to spring-clean, dusting, polishing, and rearranging furniture. I pared back clutter and lit aromatic candles so that their fragrance wafted through the house. I was creating not only a fresh energy, but welcoming an entirely fresh direction.

Today, I teach emotional resilience and qigong, and I am a shamanic practitioner. My connection to the Universe is ever stronger and more trusting.

—*Sahil Raina, shamanic practitioner, Bangalore*

Forgiveness, Part I

I was struggling with a relationship in my extended family; this person betrayed me in a way that left me shattered, and it took years to recover. She also happened to have unusual first and middle names. Think: Clementine Willa.

Clementine and I didn't speak for years after the betrayal; the hurt remained raw. Then I began to notice signs that connected me to her. First, an overheard conversation mentioned her first name. Then an obscure song I associate only with her played on the car radio. But two much bigger signs were about to unfold.

I met a woman called Willa. That piqued my curiosity. As she shared some stories about her family, she remembered how her mother would call the children's names from the porch. "Clementine, Willa, come in!" she'd say. "Clementine, Willa, it's getting dark." I was floored. What were the chances that the woman and her sister would have the same unusual names that, in their birth order, formed my relative's name?

It shook me, but even so, clearly the Universe wanted to underline its message. That weekend, I attended a workshop at the local community center. There were three first names on the student list: Clementine's, mine, and another relative connected to the betrayal.

I finally wrote her a note, telling her I forgive her.

—Radhika, Bunbury, Western Australia

Forgiveness, Part II

I was shafted by my brother over our parents' will (or, to be specific, my father's will, as my mother had died many years before). It wasn't a king's ransom, but it would have eased things for sure.

Two years down the track, I was still triggered. By then, I had moved out of state for work, and my new friends knew nothing about the situation. But all the same, I started getting messages on forgiveness.

The closet of the room I rented had a yellowed paperback on the topic. Then a colleague in the breakroom mentioned a viral post on forgiveness out of the blue. There were a few more messages, but the one that got me out of feeling stuck happened while I was having a late lunch at my desk. I flicked open a magazine and turned away for a minute. When I turned back, a headline was highlighted by a strip of sunlight filtering through the vertical blinds. It said: *The Art of Forgiveness.*

It was time to release expectations—that I would ever get an apology, or be compensated. If I didn't, I would pay an even bigger price.

—Amira, former middle school teacher, Columbus, Ohio

A Bouquet with a Message

I had been struggling with the decision to make a lateral move in my career: it didn't offer a pay raise or even a better title, but there was more scope for long-term career progression. I talked to God on the drive home one Friday night. I was tired of feeling stuck, but still unsure how to move forward. "Send me a flower from your Heavenly Garden," I said, as I pulled into my driveway. This is a popular way of asking for a sign.

Less than an hour later, there was a knock at the door as I was making dinner. I was startled to see my neighbor standing there with a bunch of flowers! I didn't quite know what to say, as we didn't know each other well; we were more on waving terms. "I've just received these," the woman said, "and I'm flying out of town for the weekend. Would you like them? Seems a shame to have them sit in an empty apartment."

I had my sign and found the courage to make a decision. I moved from limbo to sure ground, and while the adjustment in the new position took some time, it was well worth it.

—*T.S., Santiago de Chile (translated)*

Releasing a Relationship

I had been in a relationship with a woman, but the ways things had shifted felt painful and unclear. I was reflecting on this when several butterflies appeared. They remained in front of me, and it was beguiling. As I watched, I realized that while they were weaving together at times, they also fluttered separately to explore their surroundings. The parallels with my relationship hit me; we would always be connected in a sense, but it was time to let go. It was time to step back and to allow each other space.

This blend of autonomy versus dependence was a huge lesson to me. While there were many reasons to stay, I had complete awareness of what this would mean. The butterflies embodied these realizations; they symbolized transformation and rebirth. In allowing a part of myself to die, I was ushering in renewal. My mind and body were in complete synch.

In releasing this person to her journey, I was also creating space to welcome in someone else to my own.

—*Sahil Raina, shamanic practitioner, Bangalore*

Forgiving the Unforgivable

I had been living abroad in Oman for a year and was going home to Cape Town, South Africa, for my first vacation.

I had been raped more than a decade previously and had never thought much about the rapist, who was given a twenty-five-year prison sentence. I have no idea why I decided to contact the authorities to find out his status, but I was advised that he was due for a parole hearing *the day after* I arrived in the country. Coincidence?

Also, the law had very recently changed, allowing victims of serious crimes to attend parole hearings. The Universe had spoken—I simply had to go. And I did, against the advice of my family and friends.

I was the first person in South Africa to attend one of these new parole hearings. I went, and I forgave the rapist.

This has led me to what I do now for a living, which is to help people recover from their trauma and learn to forgive.

—*Lois Wagner, coach and author of*
Walking Without Skin, *South Africa*

PART II

Signs

DURING TIMES OF LOSS

CHAPTER SIX

On the Precipice

SIGNS OF IMMINENT TRANSITION

*H*ow might signs from departed loved ones keep us on our path? Wouldn't any such sign have more to do with them than with us? Well, yes and no. When we grieve, we are naturally in a deeply vulnerable place. We feel raw, as if our protective coating has rubbed off. When we receive a sign of love and connection in this state, it can register deeply—and sometimes it can arrive before the moment of death. Noticing a magical synchronicity amid grief not only helps to ease our suffering in the short term, but it also equips us for the future. A spiritual twofer.

Signs in times of pain can break open our hearts to consider new possibilities. If our beloved can find a way to send a message, what else might be possible? This can be a gateway to a different way of being. We can call on the memory of that sign in coming months and years, marveling at it. Signs often occur around moments of transition, such as a crossroads in love or career or health. In the following stories, they happen to be around imminent death. They whisper of a bigger plan and underscore the guidance available to us. Signs around the loss of a loved one can spur us to make changes in our own lives, as we are reminded of the fragility of life.

My sweet, gentle aunt would often say that when her arthritis flared up, it was a sure sign that a storm was brewing. And she was often right; it had something to do with changes in atmospheric pressure. Signs can portend change in any area of our lives, but perhaps most poignantly around the imminent loss of a loved one. We (or they) are alerted, and this can gift us the chance to leave nothing unsaid.

Other times, we see the signs in hindsight as we reflect on their departure. Often, the clues manifest not in dramatic ways, but with far more subtlety.

☺

My Experiences

The Train Is Coming

In my father's final weeks, his frailty was especially pronounced. His bones were like chalk, and his skin like tissue paper. He was almost ninety-five and ready to leave this life.

Dad had dementia, but there were still windows of lucidity which we treasured. He didn't need to know our names; it was enough that he felt loved, comfortable, and well-fed with his favorite foods.

Some days he would talk at length of life in the 1940s and '50s; I considered it a chance for time-travel and would settle in for the ride.

Then he seemed to shift from long-term memory to the present more regularly. In particular, Dad would speak of a train that was approaching, and did I have a five-dollar bill for the fare? He would scan the room as if seeing others, and the occasional flicker of his eyes suggested someone he recognized.

I was alert to this. I had read Lisa Smartt's fascinating book *Words at the Threshold: What We Say as We're Nearing Death*, and I paid close attention. I gently asked Dad where he was going, but he simply smiled. It was clear he would feel comfortable boarding that train.

My father's words suggested his soul knew what was coming, even when his physical self did not. I found that genuinely comforting. It was a loving sign from the Universe, preparing us.

Others' Experiences

Showered in a Ball of Light

I received an astounding sign just before a crucial time in my life, which helped see me through it.

I was gardening one afternoon in my yard. I had to get a lot of work done that day, as we would soon be called to the East Coast for an extended stay. I had sensed my mother was rapidly deteriorating.

I was bent over, weeding, when I saw in my mind's eye a ball of light hovering over me. It was irregular in shape, and as it came over my body, it broke up, and I was showered in this light. It enveloped me. I could see it and feel it around me. As it did, I was immersed in "a tremendous peace that passes all understanding."

Two days later, my mother passed away. Though she was elderly, it was still shocking; we hadn't known then that she had bone cancer. Just as I had sensed, we headed to Pennsylvania and stayed for a whole month. As if losing her wasn't enough, it was a frantic time overall. We had to clear out the house (no small task) to arrange an estate sale. We navigated everything required to prepare a property for the market, in a compressed time frame and amid deep grief. At the same time, I plowed through a mountain of paperwork to relocate my father to move back west with us.

It was a stressful period for everyone, but I remained calm. In fact, I sailed through what should have been a highly anxious time. This serenity lasted until I got home. I had been buffered by peace through this crisis.

—*Annette Y., Santa Fe, New Mexico*

A Major Spring Clean

I'll say it: we are a family of hoarders. We have plenty of good traits, but we hold on to so much stuff. It must grow dire before one of us will offload to Goodwill—or each other.

Last fall, I got a call from my sister, and I could tell right away she had a bee in her bonnet. Her voice was strong, and she sounded quite focused. She had been up since 4:00 a.m., thinking that her spare room was one giant junk drawer. *Well, yeah, I* thought. *What's new?*

She urged me to come over to help, but I arrived with donuts, figuring her frenzy would have passed. Not this time. She was on a mission, and by lunchtime we had piles of borrowed Tupperware to be returned, newspapers to be recycled, and bags of clothes that needed four car trips to charity.

Three short weeks later, my precious sister was gone. At just forty-one, she had a heart attack, with no family history of heart disease.

That room had been cluttered for years, and it had never bothered her. My grief counselor said that when people get a serious diagnosis, they start organizing things to retain a sense of control. I understand that, but Marnie had no idea before her heart attack. I can only assume she sensed some kind of change was looming, even if she didn't know it was her health.

—*Marnie's sister, Billings*

An Uncle Appears

My father was in an assisted-living facility when he twice encountered his late uncle. In earlier years, Dad had done the artwork for this uncle's autobiography, so they had that special connection.

Dad was an insomniac, like me. He was awake in bed one night when he saw a vision of a man in robes, looking down at a book he was reading and holding in both hands.

I'm glad he shared this vision with me, as I was able to translate it. His uncle had been a Methodist minister, and I felt strongly that the robes he wore were his religious dress. The book was a Bible.

A short while after this, his uncle again visited, though this time my father could see him only from the waist up.

This was six months before my father died. I believe that near-death awareness is not limited to the final weeks and days before we pass.

—*Annette Y., Santa Fe, New Mexico*

From Camera-Shy to Center Stage

My mother had always avoided the camera; she had bad teeth and could never afford to get them fixed. For decades we had only a few minutes of her on home video from when we were young. The footage is grainy, and the color faded. Whenever the videocam came out, she would leave the room.

When phones started to come with good cameras, she hated it (well, except to watch videos of her grandchildren). I was shocked, then, to come home for the holidays a few years ago to see her in the living room, watching our old home videos. She had called my nephew, unsure how to play them on the TV. Yet suddenly here she was, rewinding and watching over and over.

I was taken aback and asked her, "Why now?" She shrugged and smiled. I figured she was missing my dad, who had passed twelve months before. I tentatively asked if she would let me film her. She not only agreed, she went one better! My son had asked to interview her on camera for a school assignment, and she had balked. Now here she was, on the (phone) camera, talking about her childhood, the games they played, and how her parents made ends meet. It was surreal, but I decided to enjoy, not question.

That was Thanksgiving. By New Year's, Mom had joined Dad in heaven. She passed away in her sleep. I don't know if she felt some change was coming, or if her angel encouraged her to do it, but that interview with my son is a gift to the whole family. Those final weeks, we all experienced a different side of Mom.

—*Mariella F., Long Island*

Divine Help to See My Husband

My husband battled both Parkinson's disease and dementia. He needed specialty care in an assisted-living facility during the last year of his life. His dementia sparked a severe decline in cognitive abilities at the end. While we saw each other using phone apps, I hadn't seen him in person for six months due to the pandemic.

He passed on a Wednesday. On the Friday before, hospice had stopped food and water, and gave him morphine and anti-anxiety medication to keep him comfortable. In what transpired, I would come to see that in his final days, *Bob would be free of dementia,* despite his condition and the cocktail of medications that left him in a thick mental fog.

Two days later, the staff called to advise they would make an exception to current protocols and that I could see him. Of course, I had to go, but I panicked. It was such a distance, and I wasn't up to the long drive.

Right then, a friend called. It was out of the blue, both in timing and for who it was. We are friends, but we don't see each other much or even call—ours is more of a texting friendship. Not only did she call, she offered on the spot to drive me there and back. We hit the road.

I was astonished to see how thin Bob had grown. He had always had a slender face, but now his whole body was emaciated. In fact, the moment I saw him in bed, I thought he had passed already. He was so still, with his eyes and mouth closed (he often breathed through his mouth), and the room felt clean and fresh.

He had been turned to lie on his right side (he was left-handed), and I caressed him as he lay there. I told him I loved him, and I was there to walk him home (in the words of Ram Dass). I continued to talk to him, and while he could not speak back, I was aware he could understand me in a way he could not before.

I was startled that as I was talking to him, something hit my elbow. He had grasped it, even as his eyes were still closed. His left arm was the only thing that moved. He started rubbing my arm, and he would move his hand in reaction to our conversation, speeding up or down in response to my questions.

As I continued to talk, he moved his hand from my arm to my waist. I asked him if he would like me to spread his ashes on the mountain where we'd had our first date, and his rubbing became faster in agreement. I video-called my daughter to share this experience, and she too was astonished at his ability to move his left arm. As she thanked Bob for being an amazing father, his motion increased. He clearly understood.

It felt like a soul-to-soul connection. I was so joyful and happy to see him free of the confusion and disorientation of the dementia that had plagued him for years.

A final experience was yet to unfold. I was telling him that he would soon be with our dogs, Kiah and Yoda, and that one day I would join them for a nice long walk together. He motioned to his left hip, and I knew—in that way you know, when you've been with your love for decades—that it was shorthand for wanting to snuggle with me. We had spooned so often, but he had always been the bigger spoon, until now. I curled around him, and he instantly began to relax. His awareness and participation were being led by his soul.

It was a connection I will never forget; a depth of love beyond anything I had experienced before. It was so transformative that I felt intoxicated. I believe the connection came from Bob's soul.

From that moment on, I felt such joy. My husband passed on the following Wednesday, and even beyond that, the feeling of love stayed with me until Friday morning. I was at such peace now that I found myself able to comfort others in what should have been the depth of my grief and shock.

—Annette Y., Santa Fe, New Mexico

You Are My Sunshine

A dream alerted me to my Nan's final moments.

I lived forty minutes from the hospital where she was. Our family roster ensured she had at least one daily visitor. The day she passed was a Saturday. It wasn't my turn to go in, but I had a vivid dream about her that woke me up early with a jump.

I nudged my partner. He said I'd been singing in my dream, and he could make out the song "You Are My Sunshine." Nan sang that to me all the time.

When I arrived at the hospital, I could tell she was not long for this world. I couldn't reach my parents. I found out later that my grandad had suffered a fall that same morning, so this delayed their visit to Nan. I whispered in her ear that I was there, and it was all right to let go. She passed away with her hand resting in mine.

Afterward, we spent a little time doing her hair, put a rose on her pillow, and then headed downstairs to await my parents and grandfather. My dad knew the moment he saw my face. I asked to speak to Grandad alone and broke the news that Nan had passed. I assured him she hadn't been alone. That conversation is (to this day) one of the hardest things I've ever had to do.

If I hadn't had that dream, she would have passed with no one from the family with her. That song—maybe that was her calling me.

—*Julie Calliss, Perth*

Three White Cats

White cats have been sent to my family again and again. I was four when Mum and I visited a pet store to buy me a goldfish; we walked out with a white kitten. I christened him Snowy, and we were best friends. Just a year later, he was hit by a car, and my little world was upended. The pain was too profound for a five-year-old to ever articulate, only feel.

A year later, my mother noticed a white flash in our garden. It was a male cat, young and desperately thin. Mum coaxed him with food and water. In time, he grew into the spitting image of Snowy.

He continued to visit. He had no collar, nor was he microchipped or neutered. After a while, it seemed he had chosen us.

We named him Pussy. He gravitated to me, and I spent hours cradling him while he slept. He stayed with us until I finished school. Sadly, Pussy caught feline AIDS from surviving so many cat fights. His health deteriorated: his body couldn't heal, and he stopped eating.

I had a dream around this time. It was twilight in our backyard. Pussy lay on the grass, resting his head on his paw. Lying next to him was an identical cat, in a mirror pose with her head on her paw. They faced each other, inches apart. It seemed symbolic. But of what?

We made a heartbreaking decision when his suffering worsened. I patted his head and said, "I love you" until after he left us. Even so, I could still hear him purring in my head, his distinct and dignified little sound. He was telling me he loved me too, and he was now free from pain. The purring stayed with me until we left the clinic.

Six months later, Mum and I felt drawn to a pet store. We weren't ready for a new animal but craved a cuddle. There were three kittens, all white. The two males were sold; we asked to hold the female. Mum had harbored the guilt of putting Pussy to sleep, so much so that she had considered antidepressants. But when she held this kitten, the effect was instant. Mum found this deeply healing. She released the pain she'd been carrying, and when the kitten looked into her eyes, Mum knew. We brought her home.

Mum named her Aurora, a beautiful name of light after meeting her in my dream set at twilight. Aurora has been a light in our lives—unique and repelled by cuddles, unlike her predecessor. Aurora always slept on my bed. She'd snuggle into bed and head-butt my tummy. Leaving home was hard, but it was hardest to say goodbye to her.

Aurora somehow "knows" when my brother or I will be visiting. She will sit by our respective bedroom doors, usually for the twenty-four hours before we arrive. Mum knows to expect us for a meal or a quick visit.

I don't know if our cats are connected, or even if it's the same cat returning to us, but I like the idea and see it as a strong possibility.

—Belinda Zanello, Adelaide

CHAPTER SEVEN

I'm Home!

SIGNS FROM THOSE WHO HAVE JUST PASSED

*L*osing a loved one is both a universal experience and deeply personal. Our family and close friends want us to know they are fine. They seek to assure us they have arrived home to the Other Side, or to remind us in the months and years that follow that they remain close by.

It's only natural that we crave a sign in the early days after a loved one has passed. This time is surely when we're most raw and vulnerable, and we feel our separation keenly. Eventually, we must return to our lives, though we're left to move on amid a harsh new reality. We ask for messages to help ease our pain and sense of separation. The Universe acknowledges this with gentle patience. Given that love is a core part of our human experience, grief in the face of losing someone dear to us brims with spiritual insights. How we grieve, how we find meaning in heartache, and how we learn to process our loss all help to progress our spiritual evolution.

Sometimes, the grieving process is complicated by disagreements we may have had in the past. People can carry this weight for years. But when we worry that a loved one is mad at us or harboring a grudge, we're attaching an earthly emotion to the heavenly realm. They cannot feel these negative emotions on the Other Side, nor do they have any need to do so.

If you have not yet received a sign from your loved one, I want to assure you that no one is holding out on you from the Other Side. It is much more likely that they are joyfully preoccupied. On this topic, let me point you to respected authors such as Rob Schwartz, Brian Weiss, Allison DuBois, and Dr. Raymond Moody. Disclosure: I have consulted for Dr. Moody and write a column for his site. His book *Glimpses of Eternity* is a beautiful and deeply comforting read.

⊙
My Experiences

Dad's White Bouquet

As I've shared, Dad passed in his mid-nineties, and like anyone, I wanted to know he had arrived home. As I talked to him, telling him I was happy he was young again and pain-free, I asked for a specific sign. I wanted an all-white bouquet to arrive on our doorstep. As often happens at times like this, flowers did arrive, and among the colorful offerings, an all-white arrangement stood tall. We had our sign.

Granny Says Goodbye

My grandmother passed in the middle of the night, after a terrible fall from her hospital bed left her already fragile body black and blue. As we children woke up one by one, we were told the sad news. One sister announced, "I know. Granny came to me last night, and she said she had to go." Though we had all been raised to believe in an afterlife, this experience remains nonetheless deeply reassuring and comforting.

Others' Experiences

A Butterfly Lands on Her Wrist

My uncle was a sweet, kind man, and his funeral overflowed with people who came to pay their respects. After the service, we were back at home. I had a glass of wine in hand, poised to make a toast to him. As I did, a butterfly landed on my wrist. We were indoors, so it was even more startling. It caught all our attention.

—*Sarah, Adelaide*

Dad Visits

I had returned to my boarding school (Loreto Convent, Asansol, India) after being pretty sick with malaria and a side of jaundice! I hated boarding school but didn't usually make a big deal about going. This time around, I remember really not wanting to go back. I recall my dad holding me close and saying, "Don't worry, my darling, everything will be okay."

Because it was a Catholic school, the bell would wake us at 5:30 each morning for Mass. Before the bell rang that morning, I opened my eyes and, through my mosquito net, I saw my dad. He didn't say anything; he simply looked at me and slowly disappeared. I wasn't surprised or shocked to see him; I just accepted he was there. After Mass, Mother Superior took me aside and said she had some sad news for me. I said, "I know, Mother. My Daddy has died."

—*Jo G., Western Australia*

Traveling Spectacles

My beautiful husband passed in his sleep while we were on a houseboat last October. Biggest shock of my life.

A major sign I have had was after leaving my husband's wake, I realized I had left my glasses there. Not wanting to return there any time soon, I wore my backup pair. I missed my first pair, but carried on.

About two months after that horrid day, I came home to find my lost glasses on my kitchen bench! No one knew I had left them, and I lived alone.

—*Joy R., Adelaide*

ALICIA'S NOTE: In spiritual literature and parapsychology, Joy's glasses would be considered an *apport*. This term refers to the transference of objects from one place to another, or the appearance of an object from an unknown source. ■

A Photo Reveals a Surprise

My mother, Mary Brown, was born in February 1922 and passed away in February 2021, just shy of her ninety-ninth birthday.

As I prepared her eulogy, I felt so proud of her well-lived life. One of the memories she always liked to share—and one that she was immensely proud of—was her time during World War II when she helped build the Sunderland flying boats. These aircraft were specially commissioned by the Royal Air Force. She worked in the Blackburn factory on Castle Street in Dumbarton, Scotland. The factory was below Dumbarton Castle on the River Clyde.

I started looking for a picture of one of these aircrafts to include it in the photos of my mum's life. I googled "Sunderland flying boats, Dumbarton, Scotland" and up popped a picture of Dumbarton Castle sitting majestically on "The Rock," as it is called. The Sunderland flying boat was on the slip way, and the workers were gathered on the dock.

My husband spotted something from across the room. He said, "Sylvia, enlarge that photo, please." As he peered closer, he announced, "There's your mum, right in the middle." My mother is in the history books, and I have another photo to treasure.

—Sylvia Holzapfel, Adelaide (via Scotland)

The Clock Stops. A Song Plays.

When my father passed away, the battery-operated clock on the living room wall stopped working. It froze on the time he died, 11:30 p.m. The family cat stopped dead in its tracks, lingering in the hallway, and staring into nothing all night.

After the funeral, my sisters, mother, and I gathered in the living room and turned on the stereo. The radio was tuned to a program called "Six O'Clock Jukebox." Earlier that day, the funeral directors had played the wrong song as my father's coffin was being lowered into the grave. They were supposed to play Johnny O'Keefe's "Shout!" but instead played the Beatles' "Twist and Shout." We were too emotionally exhausted to bother fixing it.

While sitting around that evening, sad and grieving, we all smelled a waft of our father's cologne—Old Spice. As we looked at each other, the radio began to play Johnny O'Keefe's "Shout!"

We knew our father was still with us in spirit. We stopped crying and smiled. He was okay.

—Sher'ee Furtak-Ellis, author of
Eluding Sylvia, Chasing Poe, *Adelaide*

Millions!

Kylie was my best friend from age twelve, and we were camping with her family one holiday weekend. At the beach, we saw a little boy scooping up handfuls of sand and throwing them in the water shouting, "Millions!" We thought it was funny, and we often would re-enact it if we were at the beach or near any water; it became a private joke.

Cut to the day after Kylie died at age forty-two. I visited the wooden jetty where she had her wedding pictures taken. I sat at the end; there was a concrete path leading up to it along the water's edge, with no sand nearby. Suddenly, a bunch of sand scattered in the water in front of me as though someone had thrown it in. There was no one around, nor were there any birds.

I instantly said, "Millions!" and I knew it was Kylie saying goodbye.

—Michelle C., Rockingham, Western Australia

My Sister Visits in a Dream

I will never forget the way I heard about my sister's passing—and the dream she sent shortly afterward.

I was driving from Adelaide to Melbourne when I began to feel nauseated; it became so bad that I had to pull over to be ill by the side of the road. It made no sense. I hadn't eaten anything disagreeable, and I was in good health. Eventually, I resumed my road trip. That night, my brother called from Ireland to tell me our sister had died—three hours earlier, right when I had been feeling sick.

She had enjoyed a night out with friends and was walking home when she had been hit by a car. People assumed she'd had a few drinks and likely stumbled into the path of the vehicle; I wasn't so sure. She had been struggling to come to terms with our childhood, marred by violence and poverty, and I wondered if she had decided in that moment to take her own life. I worried about what state she was in on the Other Side. A few nights later, she came to me in a dream. She was so happy, healthy, and vibrant, seated at a dinner party of some sort. She was letting me know she was okay now and enjoying an abundance we had not experienced growing up.

—*P., South Australia (via Ireland)*

Champagne Corks Pop

My great aunt and uncle met at a school for the deaf after World War II. Years later, my aunt wore a hearing aid that changed her life, but Uncle Paul had always refused.

My aunt passed when I was in college, and I went to email my uncle my condolences. Something stopped me: *I should send him a handwritten note.* I scrounged for some notepaper, but the only stamp I could find had a picture of a champagne bottle on it. It seemed inappropriate for sending my sympathies. I asked around; my roommate almost howled with laughter when I asked if she had a stamp. I had a term paper due, and I knew if I didn't send the message that day, it would sit in my drawer for weeks. I sent it off, hoping he wouldn't notice the stamp.

A month or two went by, and I saw a letter with spidery handwriting in the mail. It was from Uncle Paul.

He said my aunt always promised to send him a sign once she got to the afterlife. She didn't fear death and talked about it openly. As they got older, she looked forward to the party in heaven that awaited her with her parents, siblings, and the little boy they had lost at age four. It would be a wonderful celebration. She knew it! She should send him popping champagne corks! "But darling, how would I hear them?" he had asked. She wasn't easily deterred. "Your ears will pop (like the popping of a champagne bottle, or high altitude)," she said, "and you will feel a fizziness in your nose" (the way it happens with soda sometimes).

A week or so after her death, Uncle Paul found himself at home, sitting quietly. The well-wishers had cleared out, and he was alone with his thoughts. His heart ached for his wife of sixty years, and he asked for a sign she was nearby. Suddenly, his ears popped. He was a bit startled but thought no more of it. Then his nose tingled, and he remembered with a rush what her sign would be. Less than an hour later, the mailman came by—with my letter. There it was: a stamp with a champagne bottle to complete a trilogy of signs.

—*L.M.R., Brooklyn*

ALICIA'S NOTE: As I'm typing up L.M.R.'s experience, I've received a note from my local post office that my sheet of fifty stamps has arrived; I hadn't expected them for another month. I've never before ordered stamps, but they were so cheerful, I couldn't resist. They show clinking champagne flutes, filled with bubbly. ■

Our Dog Mitzi

We had our beautiful dog Mitzi for eighteen years, and she was the most intelligent dog we had ever owned. She was more like one of the family than our pet. If we couldn't take her somewhere, we didn't go. When it was time to let her go, we were heartbroken.

That same night, I woke to something moving at the end of the bed. Thinking it was only Mitzi as usual, making herself comfortable, I rolled over to go back to sleep. A cold shiver went down my spine. We had buried Mitzi today . . . so who was at the end of the bed? I sat up in bed with a jolt and turned on the light. There was nothing there! "What's wrong?" my husband, James, asked. "I just felt Mitzi at the end of our bed," I told him. "Oh, for goodness sakes," he said. "Go back to sleep. She's dead, remember? We buried her in the backyard." I lay awake thinking about her for the rest of the night. It felt real.

About a month after she passed, we were getting ready to go away for a few days. I went back into the house for a final check. As I turned to go out the back door, something caught my eye. *There, sitting in the hallway, was our Mitzi.* I smiled and said, "Come on girl, let's go." I picked up Mitzi's lead which was still hanging on the hook outside the back door. My husband looked at me as I held it in my hand. "Mitzi's coming too," I said, putting her lead in the compartment of the car door. He never said a word. James always dismissed these things as utter nonsense.

Until the day he experienced it himself.

James loved his afternoon nap. He would call out to Mitzi, and they would doze together. She would always curl up near his back. About two months after she passed, James disappeared for his usual siesta.

Ten minutes later, he was standing behind me in the kitchen, looking deathly white. He could hardly get the words out. "Mitzi just made herself comfortable in my back." He was shaking. I hugged him. "Now do you believe me?" I asked. He nodded and went back to bed. Since she passed (especially the first few years), we have often felt her making herself comfortable on our bed, or caught a glimpse of her in the hall or waiting by the door.

Her visits became a little less frequent after we adopted a cat. However, we still feel she is with us. She sometimes chases the cat off the bed; I am sure of that.

—*Andrea Johns, author of*
Like a Dandelion in the Wind, *Adelaide*

Dad at the Window

Mum and I arrived in Perth to start a new life after Dad's death.

We were living with Mum's brother, Uncle Trev, and his family. Mum was washing up, and I was drying the dishes. We looked up at the kitchen window at the same time. Mum yelled, "Richard!" and I yelled, "Dad!" in unison. Uncle Trev came running!

Dad was standing on the back patio in his white suit, wearing his fedora, just watching us. He was there for just an instant and then gone—it was about ten seconds before he faded away. Neither Mum nor I were upset by his visit; we felt a sense of peace and contentment. I have not seen Dad since that day.

—*Jo G., Western Australia*

A Sign from My Cousin

My younger cousin passed away in a head-on car accident five years ago. She was twenty-three. After we attended her funeral, I came home and noticed something on my sunflower plant. It was a large moth with a black-and-white jagged pattern on it. The pattern was identical to a kimono kaftan that she used to wear.

—*Belinda Zanello, Adelaide*

A Bond Spans the Generations

Uncle Joe was my great uncle, and we had always enjoyed a close relationship. Maybe our bond began when he saved me from a snake coiled above my crib (see page 15).

Despite our vast age difference, we shared a love of photography and high-quality audio gear. As a seven-year-old, I was the only one allowed to use his beloved Sony equipment to listen to records (through headphones).

As time passed, Uncle Joe grew frailer and moved into a small self-contained unit with home services. He cherished his classical music, so I made sure to set up his stereo.

Eventually, he took up residence in a single room in a care facility. For the first time in his life, Uncle Joe had no sound system to enjoy. I was given a Sony all-in-one compact player and was surprised to discover the model was JS-xxx. (his initials). I loaded CDs from his collection. He was elated to hear his beloved classical music through new headphones in this small abode. "The quality is amazing!" he said loudly. His enthusiastic endorsement will stay with me always.

Uncle Joe sadly passed away a few years ago—on my birthday. That he exited this earth on the same day I entered it was another synchronicity.

Soon after, I felt drawn to play some music through Uncle Joe's speakers. Despite delivering years of perfect sound, that day the right speaker started making strange, distorted noises. It sounded like a garbled voice talking over the music. I'm sure this was a random electronic anomaly rather than someone "speaking" to me, but it had never occurred before or since.

Uncle Joe left me his audio equipment, including a hard disk recorder. Being sentimental, I checked for special content such as home movies. Among the recordings were two unnamed files, which required some tinkering to access. I nearly fell over when I heard Uncle Joe singing. He had recorded two songs. It was haunting to hear his voice, but I felt consolatory peace that this was left for me alone to discover, as anyone else would have either simply disposed of the device or erased all the recorded content.

—*Ihaan, IT consultant, Perth*

The Day of My Nonna's Funeral

When my nonna joined my nonno in heaven, severe storms were forecast the entire day of her funeral. The funeral director had warned us that high winds would prevent the use of a marquee to shield the congregation and the committal site. I prayed all night and next morning for my grandparents to hold off the rain and wind just for an hour, while we were at the cemetery.

The storm raged all day and through the afternoon church service. However, as we were driving to the cemetery in the deluge, I spotted the most angelic looking patch of white clouds, with sun shining through the gray sky. I said to my husband, "See those? I have a feeling they're for us, and they are going to reach us as we arrive at the cemetery." As soon as we pulled up, the rain and wind stopped, and the sun shone through the clouds. This perfect weather lasted the entire hour. The deluge started again as soon as we got back into our car.

My prayers to my grandparents were so specific in regard to the timing, and they were answered with absolute precision.

—*Sara, Adelaide*

A Chance to Heal

In my younger days, I had a boyfriend who came from the country, and he was estranged from his family. We heard that his mother was gravely sick. He wanted to avoid talking about it, as he didn't think it would be worth going back to see her in case it opened old wounds. Still, I offered to drive him to the hospital.

As I walked into her room, I smelled a sweet flowery perfume in the air. I could also sense it on his mother as I bent closer to say hello. We visited for the whole day. As he said his goodbyes, I knew this would be the last time he would see his mum alive.

We returned for the funeral. Back home afterward, we were walking silently along the shoreline when I said, "Can you smell your mum's perfume?" It was as strong as it had been the day we visited. My boyfriend stopped and said, "Yes, I thought it was my imagination, as I was just thinking how glad I was that I said goodbye before she died." He added that the one thing she'd always liked to do for herself was to wear perfume. I was so excited that his mother had come to visit us down by the sea. Even though he was not a believer of the afterlife, his sense of smell helped him to trust she was there.

—*Susie Dolling, writer, Adelaide*

Cassidi Rose

Cassidi was not just a chocolate labradoodle; he was my everything. We shared so much in our sixteen years together. When he grew sick and his final days approached, we moved back home with Mum. He lapped up the TLC we showered on him, and he gave us another three months.

In the weeks after he passed, I asked for a sign. We were looking online for a rose to plant in the garden, something that would capture Cassidi's personality. That same day, Mum asked me to drop by a store to use a five-dollar gift voucher that expired very soon; I headed there reluctantly. I arrived and went to use the Covid-19 QR code check-in with my phone—and that moment, the phone went flat. Instead, I walked over to register manually. I gasped as I saw the one name on the sign-in sheet: Cassidy Rose.

—N.W., healthcare worker, Adelaide

A Visit from Harry

Since losing my teenaged son, Harry, to a motorbike accident eight months ago, I've pleaded for a sign. A month after his passing, he'd visited me in the early morning, apparently when the veil is at its thinnest. Words cannot convey the emotional intensity of this first post-death connection. When you've lost a child, you want to know they still exist, somehow, somewhere. More than anything, I want to communicate with Harry; I'll never give up trying.

I wrote an account of that first experience and those that followed over grief-stricken months. With a sense of awe, I read countless stories of the signs other people had received from their beloved in spirit but peppered with envy and sadness. Why couldn't my child send me a sign? One medium told me that electronics and lights would be Harry's thing, rather than butterflies, birds, or feathers. I could understand that, although I still looked hopefully for number and cloud patterns, or heart-shaped rocks. Surely, these weren't too difficult?

And then an acquaintance mentioned a massage therapist she described as a "reluctant medium." This piqued my curiosity, and I booked an appointment, giving only my first name.

The massage started with dim lights in a warm, cozy room, as I lay face-down on her table. I didn't speak, willing Harry to come through. About fifteen minutes later, now lying on my back with my eyes closed, I noticed a change. I felt the therapist place both her hands on my abdomen; I was startled by a tangible heat emanating from her palms, pulsing through my body. Images of Harry flooded my mind like a cinema of memories and feelings from our life together. Time lost all meaning as I lay there, tears streaming from my closed eyes, overwhelmed by emotion and grief.

Gently the therapist spoke, explaining she'd "seen" a rabbit trapped at the bottom of a deep well of pain in my shoulder, its legs caught. "Does that mean anything to you?" she asked.

"I lost my son six months ago," I explained. She recoiled. "Oh God, I'm going to cry!" she said.

Composing herself, she continued with a chakra healing. The movie screen of my son's life had ended by now. As I lay there, I began to see pinpoints of blue light behind my closed eyelids. They danced, swelled, merged, disappeared, and flowed for what seemed a long time. At first, I assumed it was my imagination, until I remembered that a medium had told me that blue light would be a sign from Harry. I tried to conjure the blue light from the blackness—I couldn't do it. Eventually it faded, replaced by a white light. I opened my eyes as the massage ended. The therapist shared with me her sense of Harry hovering close by her right side.

She left the room, and as I was dressing to leave, I felt an overwhelming sense of wonder and joy. My eyes rested on the architrave around the door: *Harry, Harry, and Harry . . .* multiple times traversing its length from knee height to my height. They were handwritten measurements lovingly recording a child's growth. *She didn't mention she had a son called Harry,* I thought.

As I was leaving, I asked her about it, and she said she didn't. It had been part of the house when she'd bought it a couple of years before. "I have a strong feeling that I can paint over it now—it's served its purpose."

—*Anne-marie Taplin, writer, Adelaide*

My Mother and Her Phone

My mother, Rae, could never manage a mobile phone while she was alive—but she made up for it from the Other Side!

She lived in assisted care in Sydney, and I am in Adelaide. Often when I tried to call her, she would have forgotten to charge her phone, or had misplaced it. It became a bone of contention between us. No one else seemed to have a problem getting through, just me. I would resort to sending messages through the staff. She was an exceptionally spiritual woman, and she had variously been a Tibetan Buddhist and later a Christian. She'd tease me, "Don't come looking for me after I'm gone, okay Frannie? (I'm a psychic medium.) Don't try to hold me back!"

The night she passed was a shock. While she was elderly, she was in hospital for a routine procedure. However, they did not take into account her heart condition, and complications arose. In the hours after, our phones ran hot with calls and texts as the family digested the news.

Suddenly, my phone started acting up. It kind of froze. Numbers were stuck onscreen, and no matter how many times I pressed, it stayed frozen, yet the alphabet font continued to change size and style. The letters and numbers appeared to glow; they literally glittered and operated as though they had a life of their own. I had never experienced this before (nor since). I was already emotionally overwrought, and my frustration grew. Then a photo appeared onscreen of my mother and me; I have some three thousand images stored. The photo began changing size, getting bigger and smaller swiftly before my eyes. Then a second image randomly appeared (again, one among thousands in my gallery). It was an angel, pointing up to the sky with ribbons of light all around her (some of Mum's friends called her Radiant Rae).

I finally realized: she was laughing, showing me all she could do with the phone, things that she could never do while she was alive. Best of all, she was letting me know that she was 100 percent fine!

Mum sent a few more messages. My brother used to call from South Africa every two weeks to talk to her. Lines of random text (from old text messages) would appear and when put together, they would form a message. She wanted my brother to know how sorry she was that she didn't get to say goodbye, and that she loved him.

—Fran Tomlin, psychic medium, Adelaide

A Blue Budgie Visits

Uncle Joe had a blue budgerigar he called Danny Boy. He adored that bird.

When Uncle Joe passed, his son and grandsons were not able to fly into town, and the service was livestreamed. His grandson Aaron was watching the memorial when he heard a noise at the front door. As he opened it, a blue budgerigar flew straight at him and into the house. The bird was tame and calmly moved around, as if he was familiar with the home. It showed no fear, even sitting on Aaron's shoulders and then perching on the laptop itself as if watching the livestream.

Was this the spirit of Uncle Joe in a new incarnation of his pet bird? Was he visiting his grandson during his own funeral on the other side of the country?

At Uncle Joe's request, his service featured the song "Danny Boy." The closing verse talks about dying and crossing a stream to be greeted by angels.

Afterward, Aaron checked with all their neighbors; no one had lost a friendly budgie. The family kept him and named him Stanhope (Uncle Joe's middle name). Stan would fly around the backyard, then return to his cage. He continued to do this when the family moved house, but one day he did not return. Upset, Aaron posted on social media. He was relieved to hear from a man who had found the bird some distance away. Aaron made a three-hour roundtrip to bring Stan home.

About two weeks later, Stan became ill. He stayed overnight at the vet and seemed to rally. He returned home, but sadly passed away in Aaron's hands shortly afterward.

The next day, Aaron received word that his grandmother from the other side of the family had died.

—*Ihaan, IT consultant, Perth*

Treat Yourself

My sister had been the lighthearted one. She would spend her allowance in a day. I'd save mine, and she'd tease, "Treat yourself!" It became our private joke.

She had been a pastry chef and had loved what she did.

But the lightheartedness came with a depressive side. My sister took her life at twenty-eight, and it tore my family apart. Everyone retreated into their corners, too broken to help each other. We all wanted to get the funeral over and done with, to just cocoon. We didn't grow up with religion, and I wasn't sure where my sister was, or how she was feeling. I asked her to let me know she was okay.

I headed out for some fresh air. In the lobby I was stunned to see a woman in a chef's outfit: the white tunic, the puffy hat, the whole nine yards. I caught my breath as she offered me bite-size pastries and said, "Time for a treat?" She had Lana's hair color, eye color, her build—even the same jaggy tooth. It turned out to be some promotion for a patisserie opening in the neighborhood, but I know it was my sister sending a message.

—*Marika J., New York City*

Gussy

Gussy was a west highland terrier, and his arrival in my life was guided by the Universe. At the time, I worked internationally, so having a dog simply wasn't practical. Still, I kept seeing a series of whimsical ads. In one, a woman sat astride a vespa and sported a helmet and scarf; her pooch was perched on the back, dressed identically. In another, she enjoyed a massage while her terrier reclined on the next table. I announced to my partner: "We're getting a dog. And his name is Gus."

Gus came to us through a comedy of errors. The breeder was certain we'd met; we hadn't. She set aside her rigorous selection process, and insisted we take him. Gus was part of our lives for fourteen years. I couldn't have children, and he truly was my baby.

When his time approached, my sister and niece flew in to be with me. I held Gus for three hours after he passed, and I treasure that time. Afterward, we took a drive to clear my head and to show my family around. I silently asked Gus to show Mummy he had arrived home.

We headed to the picturesque Adelaide Hills and returned via the airport. I was taken aback to see a billboard featuring a terrier just like Gus, looking down at me. We had been to the airport only days before, and the billboard hadn't been there. Moments later, we rounded a corner, and there was Gus again, sitting to attention on a bus ad. My boy had let me know he was over the Rainbow Bridge.

—*Judy Myers, life coach, Encounter Bay, South Australia*

CHAPTER EIGHT

I'm with You Still

SIGNS FROM THOSE LONG DEPARTED

O f course, we don't grieve a loved one only in the first few months after their passing. Nor do we confine our memories to their birthdays, or holidays, or anniversaries.

We also know that grief is not linear; it can't be put on a time-table. In the months and years that follow their death, we can feel the shock or pain begin to soften—only to experience searing heartache at the most unexpected time. What may seem the most unrelated or random thing can trigger a wave of grief at their (physical) absence in our lives.

A little reassurance can take the edge off our sharpest pangs of loss. It can be deeply comforting to know that while our loved ones are no longer with us physically, their energy remains close by.

Consider some of the signs you will encounter in this chap-ter: a dying friend keeps her promise to return and share what heaven is like; specific dates show up online and correlate to a family's special occasions; and bereaved parents are shocked to see a photo of their son on international TV!

These signs are as wide-ranging as they are personal. And a memorable one for me involves one of my father's favorite songs, in an unlikely setting.

My Experiences

A Sign from Dad . . . in a Bakery

Sometimes a sign can hit you with such precise timing that it stops you in your tracks.

It was summer, and we had been looking forward to a lovely afternoon at the home of some new friends. They lived in a part of town we weren't familiar with.

Jon woke up feeling unwell, and through the day he became worse. It was too late to cancel; I would need to drive there myself. I'll admit I was born without the spatial gene, so when the GPS malfunctioned, I could feel my stress skyrocketing as I drove over. I talked to my angels and my father, asking them to help me.

The stifling heat that day made things even more difficult, and I needed to find a particular patisserie before it closed. I finally got there and headed to the restroom. As I was walking out, I stumbled and broke my shoe. It was the final straw; I sat down at the nearest table and promptly burst into tears. A startled waitress brought me a glass of water. At that moment, a friend called me, and she patiently listened to me vent.

As I hung up, I was surprised to hear an old tune I have always associated with my father. "What a Wonderful World" speaks to small joys and the inherent goodness of life. I thought to myself, *Dad, is that you?* Seconds later, I heard my thoughts spoken aloud: "Dad, is that you?" A young woman nearby was pointing to her father's phone and asking if it was playing music. It was. The song was coming from his phone. They were surprised and puzzled; I was grateful.

It was such a calming sign and helped me to feel centered and supported. The angelic realm can bring about unlikely events to catch our attention. And our loved ones can, too. I'm delighted to say, Dad hasn't been shy in coming forward from the Other Side.

Dad Shows Up in the Movie Credits

I believe our loved ones stay close to us, radiating love. I further believe they can hear us, and long for us to know they are near.

I was watching the movie *Analyze This*, with Robert De Niro and Billy Crystal, when I was jolted by a sign from my father.

I had been thinking of him through the movie and then, right at the end, Tony Bennett sings a song about sitting on a rainbow. I smiled; Dad liked the old crooners, and perhaps like you, I've always associated rainbows with signs from heaven.

As the credits rolled, I said out loud, "Oh, Dad, we miss you."

At that very moment, his name (David Young) appeared in front of me on the credits in big letters. I gasped and grabbed my phone to snap a photo. (You can see it at **soulplans.net** and **aliciayoung.net**.)

As if that weren't enough, Dad's name was listed under the production crew as an assistant film editor. The day before, I had been researching a job in television production.

Scrambling Home from NYC

It was March 2020, and I was in New York City as concerns mounted over the global pandemic. Manhattan was a ghost town. Jon and I would speak daily; he is normally a rock of calm, but I could hear the concern growing in his voice. The Australian government had announced it could soon be closing its borders.

Always willing to call on a close contact in heaven, I spoke to Dad and asked him to get me home. After more than six hours on hold (!) to the airline, I scrambled from New York City to San Francisco, one of only half a dozen passengers on board.

I camped out in California, waiting for a flight back to Australia. At last, I touched down in Melbourne and waited for my final leg home. I was exhausted, jet-lagged, and silently thanking Dad for getting me home.

At that moment, I glanced down at my boarding pass.

It was March 25: his birthday.

An Old Friend Drops By

As I've shared, my Auntie Grace was a nun. She was close to another religious sister, who developed cancer in older age. As her friend's prognosis proved bleak, the woman accepted it gracefully, and the two shared many discussions around death and dying. My aunt could be frank, but she also had a playful side. "Of course, we believe in heaven," she said. "We've been nuns for half a century. But when you get there, will you come back to tell me what it's like?" They often laughed about that.

Five years after her friend's death, Auntie was getting ready for bed. She told me that she knew she wasn't dreaming, because she was fiddling with a broken button on her nightdress and had made a mental note to get it repaired the next day. Something made her look up, and there was her friend, sitting on her bed. "Child, she was as solid and real as you are, right in front of me," she said.

"Is it really you?" she asked the figure.

"Of course," answered her friend. "I remember our conversations and my promise to you."

Auntie found her voice and implored, "What is it like? What is heaven like?"

Her friend smiled. "It is a thousand times more beautiful, and a thousand times more tranquil, than we could have ever imagined as humans."

I sat in silence for a moment. With Auntie Grace being a teacher as well as a nun, everything had a moral. "Child, what is the lesson in all this?" she asked.

"Are you kidding, Auntie? If it takes a *nun* five years to get to heaven, what chance do I have?"

A Startling Message on New Year's Eve

It was New Year's Eve, and TV coverage of the New York City ball-drop played in the background in our home. Suddenly, a story caught my eye. It recapped an event that had happened to a couple on December 31 the year before.

They had been on the sofa enjoying the televised concert and the banter between the program hosts. Both welcomed some levity after a difficult year; their son Tim had passed away, and naturally, they often talked about him. As the clock crept toward midnight, they wondered aloud how they would get through the next year without him. His mother asked for a sign that he was all right.

Imagine their shock when, seconds later, Tim's face appeared on their TV screen! There was no mistaking their son: there he was in a photo from his preteen years. The image was part of a story on child models who had become famous—and there, in front of their eyes, was a throwback photo shoot of their son among a group of boys. It was a powerful, unforgettable moment that registered deeply for these grieving parents.

Others' Experiences

Playing with Lights and Lamps

I think we just had a visit from Jasmine. I was in the kitchen, Ben was in bed, and Nathan was playing on his computer game. Ben called out, "Don't turn off my light."

I went to his room, and both his lamp and his fan had been switched off. I asked Nathan if he did it, but he hadn't come out of his room. I went over to check the outlet, thinking that maybe the safety switch had tripped or the plug was hanging out, but no. Both fan and lamp switches had been turned to the "off" position. Then Ben said, "Hello, Jazzy. I love you. Please don't turn off my lamp." I had goosebumps.

—*Jazzy's mama, Perth*

A Visit from My Children

Before my three children were born, I had three babies who were stillborn, each in my second trimester. The first was a boy, then came the twins (a girl and a boy). I then had three more children who lived. These are also a son, a daughter, and another son, although no twins.

One evening when my children (aged about ten, eight, and five) were asleep, I was relaxing in my living room. The children slept in two bedrooms across from each other at the end of a long hallway, while I was at the other end of the hallway.

I glanced that way and saw three white shrouded figures move—*glide*—from one side of the hallway to the other, from the bedroom where my boys slept to the one where my daughter slept. One figure was taller than the other two, who were the same height.

I was filled with awe and gratitude. It came to me that these were my departed children who were visiting their sleeping siblings. They were the height that they would have been had they lived.

—Liz Hodgman, Adelaide

Dad Comes to Calm Us Down

My family lives in Jakarta and, being in the tropics, we normally have a window open in the evening for fresh air. Whenever we see a brown butterfly flying into a room, we believe it is Dad looking down on us.

One time, I was visiting from the US. Somehow, we got into an argument after one of my sisters told Mum off in front of us. Mum was upset. In the midst of it, another sister pointed out that a butterfly had just flown into the room and landed on the edge between the ceiling and the far wall. We fell silent, and I took Mum back to her room.

The next day, my mother said my sister had apologized. We were convinced that it was our father who had shown up that night, unhappy at how Mum was treated.

The brown butterfly visited again when Mum was bedridden for a year, and also before she passed away. I couldn't be there for the funeral but was there for the special prayer a week after Mum was buried. We were told later by my brother that a brown butterfly had been on the far wall the entire time.

—Pingkan, Perth (via Jakarta)

A Message via Online Shopping

About a year after my father passed, I was struggling in a new relationship. I was dating again for the first time in years after the death of my husband, and I'd learned that the man I'd met and fallen in love with had a drinking problem. I didn't really have anyone to whom I could turn for advice, and one evening I kept thinking of my father and how much I missed him and the sense of stability and security he'd always given me. He had told me and my sister one night from his nursing home bed that he would stay in touch with us after he'd gone.

I was sad that night, so I suppose I was indulging in a little retail therapy when I sat down to order some specialty soap online. It was a company I'd never used before. As I was selecting my product, I read some reviews, which included the dates the comments were posted. The first review was posted on June 19, my sister's wedding anniversary. Another review was posted on February 28, my sister's birthday. A third was posted on January 9, my birthday. And finally, within that first handful of reviews, were posts in June and October: my parents' birth months.

It was my father sending a sign he was nearby and still loving me and my sister. By including the months of his birthday and my mom's, he was saying we're still a family like we always were and telling me he was still there with me, and I wasn't alone.

—*Laura, Asheville*

A Sign at the Dry Cleaners

My partner and I had been together for decades, and it was a running joke that he wanted me to take his name. I refused; my name is my identity. But he would playfully needle me anyway.

Last year, he died suddenly, and to say I was in shock is an understatement. I had to keep putting one foot in front of the other, and that meant keeping up with the usual errands. One day I visited a new dry cleaner, and the woman asked me my name. "Smith," I said, but I was amazed to see she had written "Jones"—my husband's name. "Why did you write that?" I said, puzzled. "They sound nothing alike." She replied, "I don't know, it just came to me."

—*Josephina, Adelaide*

A Visit from Mum

A few weeks after Jazzy died, I was looking through some photos of her. I got upset and retreated to my bed to have a good cry. I was really sobbing (my husband was at work and the boys were asleep). I felt the bed compress behind me as if someone had sat down. I put my hand out to check if it was the dog, but no one was there. Then I felt someone stroke my hair, and I instantly became calmer and stopped crying. I feel it was my mum.

When we moved house, the first time Granny (my mother-in-law) came to visit us here I was showing her around. I took her to the room where she would be sleeping. It had a photo of Jazzy hanging on the wall outside the room.

As Granny passed by me, the photo "jumped" off the wall, and I caught it. No other way to describe it. That photo is still there; it had never fallen off before nor since.

We still have the flowers from Jasmine's funeral casket. They are dried and have no smell. Sometimes, though, I can sense something flowery when I pass by them. Only occasionally, not all the time.

—*Jazzy's mama, Perth*

Pink Crystal and Radio

I had lost my parents within twelve weeks of each other, and I found myself living alone in my childhood home. Mum and Dad were no longer there physically, but they sent messages of love.

One morning I made my bed as usual before work and didn't give it a second thought. When I got home that night, I was startled to see a pink, heart-shaped crystal in the center of my bed.

Another time, I was in the kitchen when I heard the radio change to my mother's favorite station.

Each time, it was a sign they were nearby.

—Megan C., Perth

ALICIA'S NOTE: The crystal that appeared on Megan's bed is another example of an apport: an object that appears from an unknown source. The mysteries of the Universe are spellbinding. ∎

My Grandfather, the Painter

My grandfather had been a painter, and the smell of paint and sweat combined to make a distinct scent that always reminded me of him. Years after he passed, I was painting my back fence, creating a wall of sunflowers and butterflies for my children, when I asked my grandpa for help. And that's when I smelled him; there was no mistaking it.

—Tanya S., South Australia

A Hint of My Mother's Perfume

I have sensed my mother's fragrance twice in my life. We lost her when I was twelve, and she was only thirty-six. Today, I'm sixty-nine. It was the sweetest fragrance, and I couldn't place it for the longest time. One day, it hit me: it was Apple Blossom perfume. My husband smelled it too. He is spiritual also, and a Reiki master.

Another time, I heard her voice. It was my birthday, and I was at my kitchen sink, looking out the window and washing the dishes. My thoughts were roaming, and I was thinking of her. My name is Patricia Anne—friends call me Tricia, but my family calls me by my middle name. I heard her say "Happy Birthday, Anne" as clearly as anything.

I once had an opportunity to see my mother, but I couldn't do it. I was lying in bed, and I heard her voice say, "If you open your eyes, I will show you me." I kept them shut tight. But my husband, Chris, did look. He said a brilliant white light filled the doorway, but it was too bright to make out a figure; he had to turn away.

We smile when a baby is born, and we cry when someone dies. But I read somewhere that it should be the other way around: we should cry when a baby arrives in the world (for the beauty of what they have left) and smile when someone goes home (knowing what they are returning to).

—*Tricia Lock, Adelaide*

Signs from My Mother

Losing my mother six years ago has been the biggest loss of my life. We were best friends, and she was such a kind, noble, and God-fearing soul. She taught me that the most important religion on this earth is humanity.

The months after her death were deeply depressing. The pain has not lessened even now, but with time you learn to live with the reality.

I still talk to her, as I strongly believe that she is watching over me. I cannot see her, but she communicates with me through energies. The day after losing her, I started talking to her. Each time I asked for signals, lights flickered or something appeared on TV, like her name.

In those early days, I was missing her badly; I kept asking her why she had left me. While I was talking to her in my mind, my phone started ringing as it lay next to me. With a heavy heart, I reached for my phone and got goosebumps: her screen name was flashing. My mother's phone number was stored on my mobile as "Maa." My sister inherited her phone, but it is still saved as Maa.

It made no sense that my sister would be calling—she was sitting next to me, watching TV. I showed her my screen. She said that it was impossible; her mobile was in her pocket, and she had been sitting still on the sofa. She stood up and took it out—it was actually on a call to me. We stared at each other, and I told her that I had been talking to our mother moments before. That call made me so happy and confirmed that she was around me.

In the six years since I lost her, there has not been a single night when she hasn't appeared in my dreams.

—*Sach T., Adelaide*

Ladybugs

I had been going through a deeply painful time in my life.

At one point, I sent a message to Mum on Messenger asking for help. (She had passed away, but her account remained open, and it felt good to write.) The next day I went for a walk, and I felt something crawl on my face. I picked it up carefully to see what it was, and it was a ladybug. It sat on my finger for a while (longer than normal) and then flew away. In fifteen years of living on our farm, neither my husband nor I have ever seen a ladybug in the pastures. Sometimes they are in the garden near the house but never in the pastures. I wasn't surprised it was a ladybug that she sent, as one of the last gifts she left on my desk was a novelty miniature clothes peg with a ladybug on it. These two signs from my mum helped me continue to fight for what I believed.

A few months later, my life was getting back to normal, and my husband and I decided to have a high tea to celebrate Mother's Day. We had just set up on a picnic blanket on the top of the hill of our property when we noticed three ladybugs in a line on my legs. So now I have seen four ladybugs in the pastures, all related to my mum. I believe she sent these latest ladybugs to thank us for celebrating Mother's Day with high tea (which she had loved) and to show us that all will be okay.

—Mary F., South Australia

ALICIA'S NOTE: Ladybugs are said to represent healing, protection, and good fortune. An art enthusiast called Max likewise sees these dainty little creatures as a sign from her mom. Recently, Max attended an exhibition of watercolors and was feeling wistful; her mother would have loved it. When Max returned to her car, her windshield was dotted with ladybugs.

I "borrowed" the sign and asked for ladybugs to show me that a work situation would resolve itself. That same afternoon, we were startled to see our balcony screen covered in dozens of ladybugs. We have been at our house one year and have never seen them again, nor is the area known for them. Oh, and the situation resolved soon after. ■

A Pelican Circles

My mother-in-law passed from cancer, and we had gathered to scatter her ashes as she had wished. As we did, a pelican circled overhead, then landed in the water close to where the ashes had been spread. We all noticed, as pelicans had been her favorite bird.

—*M. and B., Subiaco, Western Australia*

The Face of My Guardian Angel

Lisa used to come into our hair salon with her mum. Lisa was born deprived of oxygen and was left brain damaged; mentally she was around age eight, even though she was actually in her twenties. I was about fourteen when I met her. I used to take Lisa around the shops to keep her occupied while her mother got her hair done.

She was tall and quite big in stature. When her mood changed, she morphed from a gentle, kind girl to an angry and aggressive woman. And because of her size, she was surprisingly strong. Eventually, Lisa's mother had to put her in a group home. Her physical appearance also changed around that time. Her face started to distort; her eyes sunk into her face, and her hair thinned. She died around age thirty.

A few years later, I was watching *Oprah*, and the show was about how to visualize your guardian angels while you sleep, by asking your angel to come visit you and show you what they might look like. They suggested you do this nightly before you go to sleep.

A couple of weeks later, I had a dreamlike vision of a beautiful girl who I knew to be Lisa, even though I had never seen her look like that, with no facial defects.

She said nothing, but I instantly knew she was watching over me. She looked angelic, with a beautiful glow. I knew she was my angel. I was so happy to see her pain-free. I told her mum, and she was thrilled.

—Michelle C., Rockingham, Western Australia

My Brother, the Liverpool FC Fan

My brother John had been a huge fan of Liverpool Football Club, and my husband, Mick, shared his passion. It was all they talked about when they caught up. John has since passed, and I wear an infinity-shaped pendant with his ashes in it.

Some years later, we were planning a trip to Europe and the UK. We were meeting Mick's side of the family in Spain and had a great time weaving our way through Barcelona, Vienna, and Prague, to name a few. We planned to wrap up the trip in Liverpool, of course, to see Liverpool FC play on their home turf. Throughout our travels, I stored the pendant in a zipped jewelry pouch in our toiletries bag. I felt like we were taking John along with us.

When we landed in Liverpool, we checked in at the hotel and unpacked before heading out to sightsee. Mick and I were both in the bathroom, sorting toiletries, when we heard something drop. It was my pendant! We were in shock; the pendant had been in a zipped compartment. In that moment, we both immediately said, "It's John." Mick then said, "Yep, he's telling us, 'Don't forget me. I'm coming too!'" He wouldn't have missed his beloved team.

—Jeannie Pinto, Perth

Blue Eyes

I am the youngest of nine siblings. The next one up is twelve years older than me. Number five of us, my sis Teresa, gave me a beautiful cat ornament when I was about eight. It was called Blue Eyes, and it was filled with perfume. Over the years, I must have somehow donated it to Goodwill.

Fast forward, Teresa passed and I wanted Blue Eyes back, so I searched all the secondhand stores to no avail. My darling mum passed three years later, at age ninety-one.

About two weeks after Mum passed, I was driving to a shop, still actively searching, when I had a sudden urge to drive down a different street altogether. There was a secondhand store—I went in and saw my much-wanted Blue Eyes and bought her for three dollars!

—*Joy R., Adelaide*

Ocean City Pendant

I live in New Mexico and received a sign from my mother several years after she had died. We had been remarkably close and spoke daily. Even when we experienced a rough patch in my teenage years, it was because I wanted more time with her, not less. She had taught violin and, to make extra money for the family, she had played in the orchestra at Music Pier in Ocean City, New Jersey, each summer.

I was talking to my sister on the phone and crying as I remembered our mother. After that, I drove to a pharmacy, still upset and missing her deeply. As I went to the counter to collect my medication, I was startled to see a souvenir pendant that read "Ocean City, NJ." We were two thousand miles away, in the boonies of New Mexico! Add to this, my mother was known for always wearing necklaces. Today, the pendant hangs in my kitchen. I believe strong emotions can bring on signs from our loved ones, and I had been tearful and missing my mother so much that day.

—*Annette Y., Santa Fe, New Mexico*

My Spirit Guide Introduces Himself

My spirit guide showed himself to me, and it wasn't at all what I expected. I was lying in bed when he came to me. "If you look, I will show you me," he said. "I will stand side-on." I call him Aesop, as in Aesop's Fables. I kept my eyes shut tight, but eventually I relaxed. He showed me his profile—and he had the biggest nose I'd ever seen.

Years later, I went to visit an artistic medium, who draws spirit guides. She began sketching with no input from me, then stopped. "What is it?" I asked. She paused and then said, "He's got a really big nose."

—*Tricia Lock, Adelaide*

Pets at the Rainbow Bridge

We had two beloved dogs: Yoda was an eighty-pound Labrador–border collie mix, and Kiah was a chow–border collie mix. After they passed, I was so heartened to receive visits from them both, and they each happened in broad daylight.

Yoda had a distinct sound he made when he wanted my attention. It wasn't a bark or even a yelp; I find it hard to describe, but it was unique to him. I marveled that every day at precisely three o'clock he would make that sound. It usually meant he was hungry, and in the morning that same sound meant he needed to head outside.

One afternoon, I was in our hallway, when I felt the unmistakable presence of Yoda by my side. And then I heard his signature sound. It was beautiful.

Another time, it was Kiah who came through. She also lived to a good age, with all its problems. She once had a luxurious coat, but by the time she passed, she had lost a lot of hair; we could see the skin of her tail. She was skin and bones.

Kiah came in a vision; it was daytime again, and I was awake. In her visitation, she was young, exuding energy, and with a thick, glossy coat once again. We were in a beautiful green field, and she was running toward me. She didn't reach me, though, and I believe that was because it wasn't my time.

My sister said that our pets go to the Rainbow Bridge, playing there until we too cross over. Then, they stop their play and zero in on us, bounding over in joy. The power of Kiah's visitation amazed me. It came to me, unbidden.

—Annette Y., Santa Fe, New Mexico

Moving On

I was heartbroken to say goodbye to Gussy, my cheeky west highland terrier.

Each morning, we would mediate together; I mean that. I would sit on my favorite chair, and he would curl up at my feet. We would do a mediation where we descended a staircase, and it would open up to the most wondrous Garden of Eden. I would relax on a bench to take in the beauty, and Gussy would hop up next to me.

After Gussy passed, he continued to show up each morning in our garden, and I drew deep comfort from his visits. *I would even feel his fur on my face.* This went on for six months, and helped me to adjust to life without him. One day, I was surprised to discover Gussy didn't join me. It was sad, of course, but I knew he was telling it was time to move on. He would always remain in my heart.

Friends had been encouraging me to get another dog, but I resisted. Soon after, we met Ralphy, and I noticed in the paperwork that his father was born on the same day as Gussy. A friend took Ralphy's brother from the same litter. Over time, this dog showed many of Gussy's mannerisms.

—*Judy Myers, life coach, Encounter Bay, South Australia*

Fields of Yellow . . . or Gold?

My mother doesn't dream vividly, and rarely recalls them, so we took notice when she shared an especially memorable dream.

My labradoodle, Cassidi, had passed a few months before. Mum dreamed she was running with Cassidi in a field of yellow, "but not a canola field," she said. They seemed to each be a "presence" or being. Their energy was undeniable. It was joyful.

At work, I switched on the computer. It generates random screensavers that change daily. I was startled to see a field of yellow! The whole day, the phrase "fields of gold" played on my mind. Then I recalled that "fields of gold" might be lyrics of some sort. I searched: it was a song written and sung by Sting, and later recorded by an artist called Eva Cassidy. My Cassidi was reaching out to tell me he was okay.

—*N.W., healthcare worker, Adelaide*

PART III

Signs

THAT DELIGHT AND INSPIRE

CHAPTER NINE

Earth Angels

The Universe has everything—and everyone—at its disposal. With almost eight billion people roaming around, they can prove useful and convenient ways to deliver a message. The beauty of an earth angel is that they can appear at any time, whether we ask for them or not. They might provide practical assistance, emotional support, or make a random suggestion that unlocks a challenge we're navigating. And perhaps the best part? The only prerequisites are an open heart and mind. I smile to think that sometimes earth angels are completely unaware of the role they have played in our day or our lives.

My Experiences

Newsroom Tour

I was starting my first full-time job in a newsroom. The environment wasn't entirely foreign; I had worked casual shifts there as a reporter. But now, this Monday morning, I was part of the team in a way I hadn't been before. The stakes felt higher.

Carolyn was a senior reporter, respected and experienced. She had probably seen more new colleagues traipse through than she cared to remember, which makes it all the more memorable that she would make time to give me an in-depth tour.

We covered the newsroom, the editing bays, and the camera area in a way my previous short stints hadn't afforded. Then came the cafeteria. But I was a little surprised when she beckoned me to follow her inside the women's restroom. Surely it was enough to point and continue?

"See that far stall?" she said. "One day, a month or so from now, you're going to find yourself in it, crying your heart out about something you're convinced will ruin your career. When you do, come find me, and we'll have a chat." I've been a journalist more than twenty years now, and her grace and insight remain imprinted in my mind.

Some people find themselves guided by the stars, others by their gut. That day, Carolyn was guided by kindness, and it has stayed with me always.

A Miniburger—Minus Beef

Sometimes the small things are enough to let you know you're loved and supported, and they can appear courtesy of an earth angel. I remember coming home from college one wintry night. It was freezing, and my stomach was rumbling as I awaited my last bus home. The aromas of a burger chain wafted nearby, as if to taunt me. It listed miniburgers for sixty cents, but I had only half that. I jangled the coins in my pocket as if that would make them multiply. My cheeks were burning as I headed to the counter.

"What would you like?" said the girl behind the counter. "A miniburger—minus beef, please," I said in almost a whisper. She was startled and asked me again. "A miniburger, minus beef." I was essentially ordering a hot bun with two slices of pickle and a squirt of ketchup. She had to call over her supervisor, unsure how to ring up this meager sale. The older girl saw the sum of my coins and said, "Oh, it's thirty cents." She slipped me a small serving of fries, and I'll never forget how grateful I felt—and how good they tasted.

Others' Experiences

"Go See Bill"

I woke up one Saturday morning with a strong urge to check on my friend "Bill." I shrugged it off; it was early for any day, especially on a weekend when many of us enjoy a sleep-in. I pushed the thought aside and got my day started. But again, the feeling came back, with a sense of urgency: *go see Bill.* It was now mid-morning. Finally, I did.

I got ready and knocked on his door. I was still hesitant, and I must admit, I knocked a little gently. Finally, I gave it a good rap on the door. Bill answered, with his head down and looking sheepish. He didn't want to talk, but he could tell I was in no hurry to leave. Finally, he stepped back to let me in—and I saw it. "Thank you," he murmured. He had been holding a knife, summoning the courage to take his life. He was shaking; I held him like a child.

—P., South Australia (via Ireland)

A Call, a Car

Have you ever seen those billboards on the interstate that say "Donate Your Car!" and wondered who got the vehicles? Well, my husband and I did, and it changed our lives.

Phil had been battling severe back pain for years, and eventually he could no longer do his job. We struggled along (Midwest stoicism and all), but then he got a cancer diagnosis. The light in his eyes went out that day.

We let things slide, and car maintenance was one of them. Eventually, our trusty vehicle died on us. I was so stressed; our town is not known for safe or reliable public transport. Phil attended regular appointments at the hospital. The bus connections never seemed to work right, and we would arrive exhausted.

I did all I could to stay upbeat and strong for my husband, but our situation was eating at me. One week was especially tough, and I called out to God and the Universe over and over. "You can see how hard we're trying. Please help. We're getting steamrolled here." I needed a sign that things would ease.

Three days later, we got a call from the hospital. I almost didn't answer because it was a different area code. A social worker at a regional clinic had news: some locals had donated their sedan to a nonprofit she was connected to—were we interested? Were we! We met the couple the next day and left with new wheels. We were on the road for the first time in four years.

Phil passed away three years later. I still have the car, and it helped me to get work when I had to support myself.

We got more than wheels that day. I got my connection back to the Universe. We hadn't been forgotten after all.

—*Midwest widow, Iowa*

Taxicab to the Rescue

It had been a great night on the town. I broke away from the group and began to make my way home. I thought nothing of it when I noticed a cab with people waving; they seemed to be waving at me. Both the driver and his passengers were gesticulating wildly at something behind me. They had noticed a man shadowing closely behind. The taxi pulled up by my side, and the guy fled. They insisted I jump in the car and took me home. I felt so relieved, and protected.

—Trenna, South Australia

A Witness Lends a Hand

I was working in my yoga studio when a stranger knocked at my door. He asked, "Is this car your car?"

I said, "Yes, why?"

"Because a car just bumped into your car, damaging it, and this car left without leaving a note. But I saw everything, and I took a picture of the license plate."

What are the odds?

The guy who damaged my car was a neighbor. He had destroyed my vehicle and just left. But the Universe made sure there was a kind witness and sent him to me.

A few weeks ago, again: I discovered my car with a deep scratch on the hood. I was upset, mostly because it's a leased vehicle. The scratch meant I was going to have to pay €500 from my own pocket to redo the painting of the hood.

But when I told the concierge, he looked up at the video recording and immediately saw that the *only* camera in the parking garage had filmed the moment when a big construction truck hit my car and scratched it.

Again: What are the odds?

For me, these stories tell me that God has my back. He, She, or It is always there for me.

—Marion Monce Piekarec, intuitive life coach and
master Reiki healer, Monaco

A Life-Changing Encounter at a Post Office

I was rushing to mail my application for a $5,000 scholarship before the deadline next day. I struck up a conversation with a woman ahead of me in line and discovered I was short of the money I needed for express delivery. She gave me twenty dollars, even as I protested, saying, "It's not a gift. It's not even a loan. It's an investment in who you are." I was blown away. I got the application there on time, and I won the scholarship!

—*C., businesswoman, Houston*

A Mouse Roars

A shy, young office temp saved me from terminal embarrassment at work.

I had returned to my job after a too-short maternity leave. I was running on fumes, plus I was distraught to find that a difficult labor had left me with weakened bladder muscles.

One day—still my first week back—I was mortified to find I had wet myself through. I was in tears in the restroom, when the temp walked in and heard me crying. Suddenly, this timid nineteen-year-old sprang into action and took charge.

First, she thought to post an "Out of Order" sign on my stall. Genius. The door was full-length, so as long as I kept quiet, no one knew I was there. Then she "ran an errand" and raced to a department store for a plain black skirt and underwear (remember, we had just met a day or two before).

And the best part? She squeezed my hand and said, "I'm so glad you're feeling better. We don't need to talk about this again." Whoever raised this girl, I could hug you so hard right now. And her, too, of course.

Today, people race to post on social media when they do something nice. This girl? Not a word.

She was at our office that one week—perfect timing. What if she had been a permanent member of staff? I would cringe whenever I saw her. The Universe took care of that by sending a temp.

—Mama of twins and one angel baby,
Charlotte, North Carolina

Stranded in the Outback

I began my bush trips as a teenager on a 1938 600 cc single-cylinder Triumph motorbike and sidecar. The sidecar was usually packed with camping gear, and the passenger perched on top (highly illegal today).

We ventured thousands of miles across the Australian outback. Roads were mostly unpaved then—often rough and corrugated. After each trip, I routinely checked the old bike and sidecar for loose parts or damage.

One time, I noticed a clip on the chain connecting the link had come half-off and was hanging down. How it hadn't fallen right off completely was a miracle. Had it done so, the whole chain would have dropped off and I could have been stuck goodness knows where.

I wanted a spare connecting link, but the gent behind the store counter said, "Diamond chains (an American brand) are as scarce as hens' teeth—there are none available in South Australia." He explained this foreign brand was wider than the local variety and that I'd be extremely lucky to find one.

Case in point, it took him a month to locate what I needed. I snapped up the link and stored it in an old cash box, along with extra nuts and bolts, which I kept in the trunk of the sidecar.

There it sat for three or four years. Eventually, my trusty old Triumph fell to bits and went to a wrecking yard.

First, though, I removed the battered old cash box and stashed it in a toolbox under the seat of a 1954 Land Rover I had bought to continue my bush trips. This new vehicle served me well, covering ground through the Northern Territory, far west South Australia, and northwest New South Wales.

We were on our way back from the Warrego River on the Queensland–New South Wales border when we decided to take a shortcut home. This was unusual; we would normally wind through a string of towns.

On one isolated stretch, we passed a disused uranium mine known as Radium Hill. We had heard there was an abandoned maintenance track that followed an old power line down to the River Murray. The track cut through 125 miles of salt bush and scrub; it was rarely used and overgrown in places. We saw no other vehicles until halfway down, when we spotted a chap on a motorbike.

We pulled over to check if he was okay. I could hardly believe what he told us: "I'm in big trouble. I've lost the connecting link off my chain, and it's a Diamond chain, which is rare. The links are virtually unavailable."

I immediately remembered the old cash box under the seat and quietly returned to the Land Rover. I rummaged through the nuts and bolts and, sure enough, there was the exact Diamond connecting link he needed.

I walked back to the chap and held out the link in my palm. I asked casually, "Is this what you're missing?"

We were all astonished.

PS: About forty years later, I shared my experience with some bikers in a campground in Queensland. One of them recalled this same story from a motorbike magazine. The article featured a chap who had been stranded in the remote outback, where he had lost a rare Diamond connecting link from his bike chain. The only vehicle to come by had been a Land Rover—and inexplicably, the driver had the exact motorbike part he needed.

—Tony Bacon, Kingston Park, South Australia

ALICIA'S NOTE: The Universe brings people across our path at opportune times, and in turn, we ourselves are fortuitously placed across the paths of others—as the stories above and below illustrate. ■

Counseling a Repairman

Our air conditioner was giving us trouble, and a friend suggested a repairman. When he arrived, we got talking and, despite never having met him before, Travis shared quite a lot about some concerns for his son. He knew he related to him differently than to his other children. He also knew that other factors played into it: namely, Travis assumed his son was so much like him, he had a hard time seeing his boy as an individual. Travis also didn't want to repeat the same patterns his father had used to engage him growing up.

We talked for a good ninety minutes—for way longer and way more in-depth than you'd ever expect when you book a repairman.

Travis got in his car to go home and was astounded at the song that played: it had a direct bearing on the solution he sought with his son. So did the second song. And the third. By this time, he was crying and had to pull aside. Then it hit him, again: not only did each song hold a message, but each tune was the favorite of one of his children.

—Alice Bacon, coach and creator of
Your Six-Second Autopilot™, Adelaide

With a Little Help from My Friends

My friend Judy Martin was an earth angel when I lived in New York City. We shared an office. I was based at the Canadian Broadcasting Corporation; she was based at National Public Radio. I was depressed because the love of my life had brutally left me.

Judy took me to an orphanage for kids with AIDS, and we volunteered regularly there. This saved my life. Because instead of crying, I was giving love, I was giving attention, I was dancing and playing with those adorable kids. And they gave me so much love back. I still cry and miss them so much, to this day.

Judy passed away unexpectedly seven years ago, but I feel she is still with me.

I've had many other angels in my life who helped me stay alive and well and happy. They tell me to have faith, have confidence in myself, giving me unconditional love. I feel so blessed to have had all of them.

You might reply, "Yeah, so what? We all have friends; that's normal." Yes and no. For me, all these humans were God-sent.

—Marion Monce Piekarec, intuitive life coach and
master Reiki healer, Monaco

A Flirtation

You might think this is an inappropriate thing for a mother to share, but it makes my heart swell.

My son Mateo was born with a swag of disabilities, from cerebral palsy to heart issues. He was in a wheelchair from age eight. For the most part, though, we insisted he participate in everything he could. I had to learn to not coddle him, and it almost killed me; I wanted to protect him from the world, from the stares and the judgment. But I knew keeping him wrapped up in a security blanket would do him no favors.

Mateo did well at school and in his wheelchair sports. It was a joy to see him grow in confidence. But there was one area where we could not help him: love. "Mama, why don't I have a girlfriend?" he'd ask, and it tore me up inside. He would see the girls come over to visit his brothers and wonder why he wasn't going on dates. I would look to my husband, and his eyes would be wet, staring out the window.

One weekend when he was almost fourteen, we were in a sports store, getting our boys their gear for the new season. I wandered away from Mateo and was stunned at the scene I returned to: a teenage girl was flirting with him. She was smiling and tossing her hair. She would pick up a T-shirt and hold it next to her, like she was modeling it for him, and he would nod enthusiastically. She even seemed to wiggle her little bottom at one point.

I instinctively stepped behind a rack of clothes—embarrassed to be seeing this, yet thrilled for my son. From the look on his face, he was on cloud nine. Neither said a word, but he was floating on air for days afterward. She had seen him. *Him.* Not the wheelchair.

My darling boy went to heaven just four months later. But I am so happy he experienced that jolt of mutual attraction. I hope one day that girl realizes the gift of flirtation she gave my son, right there among the tracksuits and hockey sticks.

—*Mother of four, Santiago de Chile*
(via Manchester and Hong Kong)

Stop the Presses! (Or Keep Them Running)

The memorial cards hadn't arrived for my mother's funeral, so my daughter started calling printers to order another batch—but they were all shutting down for the holidays.

Despondent, she called one last printer, who explained that the presses were scheduled to be turned off within the hour. Despite this, and the fact he was hoping to start his own vacation, he kindly agreed to keep them running. "We can't have you going without cards for your grandma."

There was no time to discuss designs, so she left that up to him. The cards were perfect, right down to the color and butterflies. (The original cards arrived two weeks later.)

—Michelle, South Australia

CHAPTER TEN

Synchronicities

Synchronicities feature seemingly magical connections or chance encounters that tickle our curiosity. They leave us scratching our heads, saying, "What are the chances?" And they needn't be monumental to catch our attention.

Synchronicities' purpose can simply be to shift us from our adult obligations to reconnect us to childlike wonder.

My Experiences

A Faded Note

All day, two friends had been on my mind: the writer Lal Perera and my niece Livinia. Both happen to be of Sri Lankan heritage, but their families don't know each other.

I was on deadline to get some updated marketing material printed, and unexpectedly, I had to head across town to a new printer.

On the way back, I passed a pop-up secondhand book sale run by friends of the state library. It was ten minutes to closing, so I popped in, filled a bag with books, and looked forward to inspecting them more closely on the train ride home.

As I pulled out the first title, a faded note fell to the ground. It was twenty-five years old, and the letter writer asked, "How is Lal . . . and what is Livinia up to?"

I stared at the note, slack-jawed. What were the odds? Often these synchronicities show up to whisper to us how we are all interconnected. It's as simple and as potent as that.

Bindis

Recently, I woke up at two o'clock one morning with a singular thought: I ought to wear a bindi again. (A bindi is a decorative dot variously worn on the forehead or in the parting of the hair.) The next day, I was recommended a book and rather than leafing through it as I usually do, I cracked it open to a random page—and saw a reference on the significance of bindis in Indian culture.

Let's Elope

Jon and I had been together less than eighteen months, but it was serious, and we were already living together. I dreamt that he kept saying to me, "Let's elope." This was the night before the Melbourne Cup ("the race that stops a nation"), yet horse racing has never interested me. I couldn't have told you the name of a single entrant before we were blanketed in race-day coverage.

I was speechless, then, to see one of the favorites was a horse called Let's Elope. I did something that day I had never done before nor since. I went to the bank and withdrew one thousand dollars (I was a college student, so it didn't leave much of a balance). I was shaking as I went to place a bet. When I got there, though, I didn't know what to do, and everything was buzzing with masculine energy and the smell of stale beer. I left.

Let's Elope won the Melbourne Cup.

And as things would have it, we did end up eloping a year or two later, followed by a church wedding.

Two Books, Connected

Last winter, Jon and I headed away for a few days to wine country, a decadent gift from my sister and brother-in-law. The day before we left, we splurged at our local bookstore. Suffice it to say, Jon and I have wildly divergent tastes: his novels always feature spies and plots to overthrow world leaders. That, or sci-fi fantasy. I enjoy nonfiction, from spiritual topics to contemporary biography. As you might imagine, there's not a lot of overlap to be found in our reading matter.

One night we were both curled up by the fire, delighting in our new titles. I was delving into Jordan Peterson's *12 Rules for Life* and would read out some parts aloud to Jon from time to time. Meanwhile, he was immersed in a novel with a character who was quoting the exact same rules for life—from the same book I was reading! We were pleasantly surprised. It was a reminder of the invisible thread that connects us all.

A Recurring Name

Sometimes a name will keep appearing, be it in a conversation or a song or even an ad.

A year or so ago, I was exploring the idea of becoming a death doula (like a birth doula, but for the end-stage of life). I attended an introductory seminar at a local community center. It was fascinating, but I wasn't sure it was for me.

At the time, I was working on a project, and a colleague suggested I interview the medium and psychic Debra Diamond. I was surprised to learn she had written a book called *Diary of a Death Doula: 25 Lessons the Dying Teach Us about the Afterlife*. Later that weekend, I was enjoying a catch-up call with a friend on the East Coast. She shared she had popped by her local bookstore and "by pure luck" saw a sign for an author talk that same day. Had I heard of Debra Diamond? she asked. I was in Australia, my friend was in the US, and we both discovered the same resource that weekend.

↺

Others' Experiences

Two Boys, One Experience

A couple I know lived in Calgary for years before moving back to Australia recently. Their normally vivacious six-year-old son's behavior had been changing. He seemed to vacillate between being agitated one moment, and pale and listless the next. One day when his behavior was particularly worrying, they took him to the hospital, where he was admitted and diagnosed with type 1 diabetes.

That same day, another six-year-old boy arrived at the same hospital. His family too had recently arrived from Calgary. He was born in the same city—and on the very same day as the first boy, no less. He was also admitted and subsequently diagnosed with type 1 diabetes.

What are the odds? The boys became fast friends, as did their parents. It seems the Universe had ensured they would meet to support each other.

—Patrea O'Donoghue, sport and exercise psychologist,
Cleveland, Queensland

A Conversation in an Elevator

I am an Austrian artist with an autoimmune disease, living in Estonia. I own two businesses, a PR agency and an innovative arts-tech NGO.

As young as nine, I was playing with meditation and mindfulness. By my early twenties, I was spiritually aware. I trained with a Chinese grand master. Clairaudition and divination skills run in my family, and synchronicities are, well, my daily bread.

The first intense one happened when I was twenty-two and desperately searching for a flat in the expensive and overly populated city of Munich. My friend and I had been looking for months to find just a room, when I got in the elevator after being interviewed by a group of students in a flat share. I was exhausted.

An older guy got in with me. He looked ordinary; there was nothing remarkable about him. All of a sudden, my inner impulse became so strong it was almost a voice telling me: *Talk to him. Ask him about a flat.* I wanted to ignore it, as always, but eventually drew him into a discussion on the rental market. Turned out he had a flat to rent, perfectly new, in the middle of town, and big enough for two girls. We lived there, happily, for the next two years, until I left Germany.

—*Anima, archetype marketer, Estonia*

An Abandoned Book

In the early 1970s, Sir Anthony Hopkins was slated to play Kostya in a film adaptation of *The Girl from Petrovka*. To prepare for the role, he set out to read the book but was unable to find a copy in any bookstore, despite a rigorous search. Then, while seated in a London Tube station, he noticed a paperback that someone had left behind. It was the very title he sought. When he opened it, he found that the book had also been signed by its author, George Feifer.

The Night Before Surgery

I've always been a level-headed gal; I'm not easily given to seeing the mystical side of life. It's something my wife and kids tease me about. But there is one experience I keep turning over.

We have three children, and our youngest was due for surgery to correct a serious stomach and digestive issue. I had mostly kept the stress at bay, but I was jittery the night before. Normally, a walk around the block would clear my mind. But I surprised myself when I remembered a local yoga class had started up again; I hadn't been in months. Yep, that was it. I would go to yoga to de-stress.

I got there a little late and found a space to hide out in the back. A woman snuck in after me and took the next spot over.

I felt stiff and out of shape as I tried to follow the class. And I wasn't the only one trying to contort myself into various positions. One sideways glance at my neighbor and we burst out laughing, to the annoyance of the teacher. We persevered a bit longer, but when she cocked her head toward the door, I scrambled to follow.

Her name was Cathy, and her warm, bubbly nature put me at ease. As we chatted, I noticed Cathy had a small port-wine birthmark near her right temple. I told her about my child's operation the next day. Would you believe, she was not only a nurse, but a surgical nurse, and she reassured me. I left soothed. Lighter.

The next morning, we were at the hospital bright and early. I stayed with my baby girl as long as they would let me, but eventually I could see the staff waiting to greet her. They wore surgical scrubs, and masks concealed their faces. Then something caught my eye: one person had a birthmark near her right temple. If her birthmark had been anywhere else on her face, I would not have seen it.

It was Cathy. We both did a double take. She said that she didn't usually work at that hospital. The nursing agency had booked her the night before—hours after we had spoken.

She had been sent. To us.

—*Maria, Sydney (via Florida and Florence)*

Grandma's Workplace

When my mother passed away, our daughters lent a wellspring of support. One organized our accommodations in Mum's hometown for the funeral. It wasn't until we arrived that I realized it was the same motel where Mum had worked in my childhood, and it was still being run by the same family. My girls were amazed; they had no idea their grandmother had worked there.

Mum had been a cleaner at the motel, and the people she worked with became lifelong family friends, with their own stories of her. We're still in contact today.

During summer school breaks, we would go to work with Mum in the morning and spend hours swimming and jumping off the nearby jetty until she finished work at lunchtime. To think: our grieving family got to stay where Mum had spent so much time and had so many happy memories. It was like she was walking beside us, still looking after us.

—*Michelle, South Australia*

———— ☙ ————

How Far Can Synchronicities Unfold?

Many synchronicities are singular events or a sequence that unfolds in the short term to reveal the interconnectedness of the Universe. Others play out over the course of a lifetime. Consider the story of the famous "Jim Twins," identical twins who were raised apart. Their experiences featured prominently in the landmark Minnesota Study of Twins Reared Apart. The parallels of their lives are staggering.

The "Jim Twins"

The Jim Twins were born in 1940. At barely four weeks old, they were separated and adopted by families who lived in different towns. These adoptive parents were unaware their boys had a twin brother. Each baby was named James, and each was known as Jim. The twins were reunited at age thirty-nine, and their meeting revealed toe-curling synchronicities.

Each grew up to marry and divorce women named Linda. Each later married women named Betty.

They chose near-identical names for their first sons. One named his boy James Alan; the other used a slightly different spelling, James Allan.

Both Jims worked in the field of law enforcement. Both had been employed as a part-time deputy sheriff in Ohio.

Both men were chain smokers, and both drove Chevrolets, as reported by *Ripley's Believe It or Not*.

Looking back to their earlier years: Both had an adopted brother called Larry. Both named their pet dog "Toy." As students, both struggled with spelling and shone at math. Both later studied mechanical drawing and woodworking.

In terms of their health, each twin developed headaches at age eighteen, and each gained ten pounds at the same stage in life. At the time of the study, both stood six feet tall and weighed 180 pounds.

Their shared synchronicities are astonishing, and speak to the unseen, unshakeable bonds between identical twins.

PART IV

EMBRACING

Signs

IN YOUR LIFE

CHAPTER ELEVEN

Asking for Signs

I maintain an ongoing conversation with the Universe. I talk through words (spoken or unspoken) and meditation, and it responds often through signs. I'd like to think that mostly I sound grateful, but sometimes I seem like a disgruntled diner in a restaurant: "This is not the life I ordered!" When our circumstances feel out of synch, we can always ask for help.

I believe you have a divine pipeline of signs ready at your disposal. Sometimes it can feel as though these messages arrive in a trickle, as if from a garden hose; other days, they come in a flood, like a burst fire hydrant. I don't believe that your supply of signs ever stops; it's more likely that you get busy and distracted, and you forget to tune into them.

Let me remind you, I don't believe there are limitations on the number of signs we can ask for, or how specific our requests should be. The world is awash in detail. If you look at a beautiful bird with a dozen different colors in its plumage, you'll see that the Universe reveals itself as a Universe of detail. That's why manifestation books ask you to get joyfully specific about what you're seeking.

Why ask for signs? For some people, asking for signs may seem a bit unusual; asking for something specific may be a bit too much. They may see it as a slippery slope, as if suddenly they'll be Spiritual with a capital S and, before they know it, they'll be dancing around a fire at midnight, worshipping fruit.

It doesn't have to work like that. Imagine for a moment that you're being sued. Someone is taking you to court for everything you have. You can't eat, you can't sleep; you're consumed by your legal woes. Meanwhile, you have a close friend who is a lawyer—yet you mention nothing to them. Just as your friend would need to know about your issues before they could help, the Universe needs you to exercise your free will by calling on it for assistance. If you talk to your guides and ask for signs, they can help with what is keeping you up at night. It's that act of asking for help—and surrendering yourself to the outcome—that unleashes angelic help.

You might recall earlier that T.S. from Santiago de Chile asked for a sign to shown up as "a flower from the Heavenly Garden." Requesting help and then receiving a flower shortly afterward—especially from an unexpected source—is said to be a sign that your plea will be answered.

I know this from personal experience. I was talking to the Universe one night, asking for guidance in taking a new direction at work. The next day, I met my friend Angelo for coffee at one of our favorite cafes. He wasn't at our usual table, but as I climbed the stairs, I noticed a huge bunch of flowers at a nearby table. *Someone's about to be delighted,* I thought. Turns out, that someone was me! Angelo surprised me with a stunning basket of purple flowers—every shade of violet you can imagine. The arrangement was so tall, I hadn't seen him sitting behind it. Sign received—in the clearest way.

Attuning Yourself to Signs

If you've never experienced the power of signs, it's time to start becoming attuned to them. Even if you have, you may need to brush up on connections that might have lain dormant. Here are a few tips:

Attuning ourselves to signs is not complicated. In fact, oftentimes we complicate something that can simply start with "Please help." We can ask aloud, or in meditation, or we can write down our request. Then we need to slow down and pay attention to what is unfolding around us.

Rituals can help. If you feel like creating a ritual around your requests, play with it and infuse joy. You might find a spot in your home, garden, or balcony that becomes the place where you set your intent. Or instead of a physical place, you might want to set aside a certain time each day. More important than the when, where, or how is simply doing what feels right to you.

Set an intent. Suzanne Thompson is a meditation practitioner based in Adelaide who designs and delivers programs around Synchrodestiny—a powerful and joyful interplay of synchronicity and destiny, which helps events unfold on our path. Suzanne works with both children and adults to infuse attention and intention around their interactions. She sets two intents throughout her day: *I don't know what I don't know,* and *I have all I need before I need it.* This ensures she stays open to signs and support from the Universe. You can do the same. It can be the difference between hoping to have a great day and actively co-creating a great day with the Universe.

Keep it casual. We can speak to our angels and guides as casually as we do our best friends. No need for "thees" and "thous," as lovely as they are. And just as with our best friends and family members, the small, day-to-day things are enough to share. We needn't turn to the Other Side only in times of crisis or momentous decisions (though that is fine, too). I often talk to the Universe about my day—be it work, or a new friendship, or our plans for the weekend.

Release the outcome. I was reminded of this recently when I learned of a setback on a major project; it was dispiriting. The information itself wasn't deadly serious, but the development still left me flat for a day or two. The morning after this news came, I was heading out to meet two girlfriends, Celeste and Mia, for coffee. On the way, I was speaking to my angels and said (quite vaguely for me), "Please send me a win. I need a win." I decided to surprise each friend with a little posy. Then it was my turn to be surprised: they had a gift for me. Mia had been helping her mother-in-law move house and came across a deck of brand-new angel cards that the elder lady had long since put aside (the very same type I have, my favorite, which are getting old and frayed). "They're from Win," she said, meaning her mother-in-law, Winifred. If that weren't enough, that same afternoon, Jon mentioned his grandmother out of the blue (whom he had never met). Her name was also Winifred. I had asked to be sent a "win." I got two Wins—*and* the angel cards.

Ask, then stay attuned. Listen from your heartspace, and don't worry if rigid logic does not apply. A sign will touch your heart and may conjure an image that means something specifically to you.

Keep a journal or use an app. Start or maintain a signs journal and look back on earlier entries every few months for recurring themes.

A playful energy helps. We don't need to beg or plead; in fact, I believe that sense of near-desperation affects the vibration around our request. A lighthearted approach works well, as Greg M. of Dayton shares:

■ My husband and I were taking an evening stroll, and we commented on how varied the homes were in our neighborhood. There was a hodgepodge of styles, reflecting trends over the last half-decade. He surprised me when he suddenly remarked, "That house would look great in whitewash with blue trim, like those homes in the Greek Islands." I laughed and played along, adding, "Yes, we need to have a home by the water one day, with whitewash and blue trim."

A week later, our property manager in Costa Rica sent us a maintenance report. We own a vacation rental home there, and the property was undergoing a raft of renovations ahead of peak season. It needed to be painted, but we hadn't discussed color schemes yet. He had gone ahead and chosen white with blue trim. The house is by the water. ■

No matter how modest, our homes represent our little corner of the world and a sanctuary from everything beyond our front door. Each night, I ask Archangel Michael to stand guard on our roof. I also send him to the roofs of friends and family. Angels are not bound by time and space as we are, so they can be with everyone at the same time.

It's your turn—and your time—to develop or increase awareness of signs in your life.

Trusting in Signs

Imagine that you have a six-year-old who comes home from school one day and tearfully tells you that she is being bullied. You would comfort her, of course. "Don't worry," you'd say. "I'll take care of it."

Would your first grader walk away, worried about the strategies you might employ or how effective they might be? Hardly. She would trust that you have it covered, and she would skip off feeling lighter.

The Universe wants us to have that same unconditional, childlike trust. When we ask for a sign, we can trust that we deserve it and trust that it will come. This is true even if it shows up in a different way or on a different timetable to what we might expect.

If you find it hard to trust in signs, consider this. A college student who was studying world religions was confused about which path was best. He went to his theology professor and threw up his hands. "Buddha. Jesus. Allah. They all sound good. Which one is best?" He was surprised when the professor offered no clear guidance. "There's no way to know," said the academic, "until you try one on, to see if it fits."

We have to try on signs, to see how they fit.

Epilogue

*A*mid this book deadline, I experienced what I believe to be time compression. I don't say this lightly; I had read about the concept, but had never encountered anything like it.

I had been trying to wrap up the manuscript when I remembered a prior commitment: I had planned to see a musician friend perform in the city. The venue happened to be next door to my coworking space, where I go three times a week. It's always a good twenty- to twenty-five-minute walk from the train station—and I naturally walk at a fast pace. I talked to my angels and planned to work on the train there and back to make up for the lost writing time.

The band delivered a great set, and I set off back to the railway station. I had already surrendered the time involved and hadn't checked the timetable back. I glanced at my watch as I left.

When I arrived at the station, I was staggered to see I had arrived in *nine minutes* and walked straight onto a departing train. It was a Sunday schedule, so I would have easily waited a while if I had missed that train.

I had noticed a sensation of gliding along, but that was it. I was not stressed nor running or puffing in any way. I was able to make it home faster and get on with writing.

The Universe helps in ways we might never anticipate.

Contributors

I am grateful for each contributor who has made time to share their experiences of signs from the Universe. Many have chosen to remain anonymous. Here you will find a list of those whom you might like to contact for their professional services. The list is organized by first name for your convenience. Regardless of location, you will find many offer their services virtually. You will also find them on social media, whether or not they have a website.

ALICE BACON is an Adelaide-based mindfulness coach and creator of Your Six-Second Autopilot™.
Visit: **alicebacon.com**.

ANDREA JOHNS is an Adelaide-based writer and author of *Like a Dandelion in the Wind*. Visit: **australianauthors.store**.

ANIMA is an archetype marketer based in Estonia.
Visit: **vitruvianvision.com** and **thesophisticatedgeek.com**.

ANNE-MARIE TAPLIN is an Adelaide-based writer.
Email: **annemarietaplin@gmail.com**.

BERNIE BEITMAN, MD, is a psychiatrist and the founding director of The Coincidence Project. He is author of *Connecting with Coincidence: The New Science for Using Synchronicity and Serendipity in Your Life.* Visit: **coincider.com**.

BEVERLEY HOLT is an energy healer, podcast host, and teacher based in Sydney. Visit: **mywellnessspring.co**.

FIN JAMES is an energy alignment mentor and intuitive guide based in Denmark, Western Australia. Visit: **finjames.com**.

FRAN TOMLIN is an Adelaide-based psychic medium. Visit her on Facebook: **@FranTomlinPsychic**.

JUDY MYERS is a life coach based in Greater Adelaide. Her clientele is women aged 50-plus.
Visit: **judymyerscoaching.com.au** and **queenagers.au**.

KATE DUNCAN is an insight meditation teacher and yogi based in Adelaide.
Visit: **kateduncanyoga.com** and **cittaretreat.com**.

KERRY TOTH is a writer and tarot card instructor based in Adelaide. Visit her on Facebook at Kerri Tothe Intuitive Tarot and Health Counselling (please note the name variation).

LEIGH WHITE is a Sydney-based transformational coach and master quantum energy healer. Visit: **leighwhite.com.au**.

LOIS WAGNER is a life coach focused on healing from trauma, based in South Africa. She is author of *Walking Without Skin*. Visit: **walkingwithoutskin.com**.

MARIA BOWES is an Adelaide-based intuitive massage therapist and healer. Visit her on Facebook: **@HeavenlyMassagebyMaria**.

MARION MONCE PIEKAREC is an intuitive life coach and master Reiki healer based in Monaco.
Visit: **elandalife.com** and **fr.elandalife.com**.

NATHAN CASTLE, OP, is both a medium and Catholic priest in the Dominican order, who works with souls stuck between realms. He is author of the *Afterlife Interrupted* series.
Visit: **nathan-castle.com**.

PATREA O'DONOGHUE is a sport and exercise psychologist based in Cleveland, Queensland.
Visit: **positivepsychologystrategies.com.au**.

SAHIL RAINA is a shamanic practitioner based in Bangalore, India. Follow him on Instagram **@RhythminChaos**.

SHER'EE FURTAK-ELLIS is a writer based in Adelaide and author of *Eluding Sylvia, Chasing Poe: A Choose-Your-Own-Adventure of Bipolar-Disordered Mood People*.
Visit: **australianauthors.store**.

SHRUTI DIWAN is a website developer based in Perth.
Visit: **shrutidiwan.com**.

SUSIE DOLLING is an Adelaide-based writer.

SUZANNE THOMPSON is a meditation practitioner based in Adelaide. Visit: **soularchaeology.org**.

TOMIK SUBAGIO is a respected, veteran translator and interpreter. He is also the longest-serving public servant in Australia.

VEATHIKA JAIN is a journalist and pottery studio owner in Brisbane. Visit: **veathika.com**.

ZOE MAC (aka Zoe Macfarlane) is an energy healer in Burleigh Heads, Queensland. Follow her on Instagram **@ZoeMacEnergy**.

Select Bibliography

Beitman, Bernard D., MD. *Connecting with Coincidence: The New Science for Using Synchronicity and Serendipity in Your Life.* Deerfield Beach, FL: Health Communications, Inc., 2016.

Bolsta, Phil. *Sixty Seconds: One Moment Changes Everything.* New York: Atria Books, 2008.

Castle, Nathan G., OP. *Afterlife, Interrupted, Book One: Helping Stuck Souls Cross Over.* C2G2 Productions, 2018.

———. *Afterlife, Interrupted, Book Two: Helping Souls Cross Over.* C2G2 Productions, 2020.

Diamond, Debra. *Diary of a Death Doula: 25 Lessons the Dying Teach Us about the Afterlife.* Alresford, UK: O-Books, 2019.

Feifer, George. *Girl from Petrovka.* New York: Viking, 1972.

Gilbert, Elizabeth. *Eat, Pray, Love: One Woman's Search for Everything Across Italy, India and Indonesia.* New York: Riverhead Books, 2006.

Jung, C. G. [Carl Gustav]. *Synchronicity: An Acausal Connecting Principle.* Translated by R. F. C. Hull. Princeton, NJ: Princeton University Press, 1973.

Minnesota Center for Twin & Family Research (MCTFR). "Other Twin Research at the University of Minnesota." **mctfr.psych.umn.edu/research /UM%2oresearch.html**.

Moody, Raymond, MD. *Glimpses of Eternity: Sharing a Loved One's Passage from This Life to the Next.* With Paul Perry. New York: Guideposts, 2010. **lifeafterlife.com**.

Peterson, Jordan. *12 Rules for Life: An Antidote for Chaos.* Toronto: Random House Canada, 2018.

Smartt, Lisa. *Words at the Threshold: What We Say as We're Nearing Death.* Novato, CA: New World Library, 2017. **finalwordsproject.org**.

Toronto, Suzy, *Behind Every Successful Woman Is a Substantial Amount of Chocolate.* Boulder, CO: Blue Mountain Arts, 2016.

Acknowledgments

I hold special affection for *Divinely Align Me,* and by extension, for the people who helped me bring it into reality. My heartfelt thanks to each of them. I realize that I have referenced a small army here, but I offer this appreciation unapologetically and with a smile.

Support Team

To Holly, for her deep wellspring of support across seven books, and for making time amid major renovations, unending research, school commitments, Christmas, and a Boo; to Laura, for the length and breadth of our spiritual deep-dives; to Chris, whose work ethic in studying full-time while working full-time still staggers and inspires me in equal measure; to Amelia, for her loving thoughtfulness, generosity of spirit, and research that is unparalleled; to Shruti, for being the highlight of the course where we met, and for her philosophical approach to life; to Meg C., who graciously shared deeply personal signs to bring comfort to others; to Angela, for so kindly providing feedback, especially since the topic held as much appeal for her as a car manual;

to Sandy, a lightworker who has enriched my life for decades; to Chrissy, for possessing such warmth and depth of kindness; to Ihaan and Tania, for their storied friendship and for their considered feedback; to Lourdie and Astor, who sifted through the gold of their life experience to share intriguing nuggets; to Pingkan, who embodies the essence of being a lady.

Further thanks to Grace C., for your generosity of spirit in once again making time to listen and read; to my cousin Jo G., who shared powerful experiences so warmly and openly; to Annette Y., for generously sharing her wealth of enriching spiritual experiences; to Leigh, for her kindness and support.

To Alice, who graciously spread the word, and whose conversations I treasure; to Angelo, for us being part of each other's tribes; to Liz, who is both a role model and a gateway to a new chapter; to Marion, whose spiritual insights have inspired me since our days in Moscow; to Beverley, who has gifted me fresh perspectives on the magic that swirls around us; to Lal, on whose counter I perch for treasured chats; to Avis, Dave and Benjamin, for opening up a new world!; to Mehul and Veathika, for their ongoing support (despite having the temerity to move to Brisbane).

Most of all, to Jon. The jangle of your key in the door will always be my favorite sound.

Contributors

Additional thanks to Alicia Geddes, Amira, Andrea Johns, Anima, Anne-marie Taplin, Bapak Tomik Subagio, Belinda Zanello, Bevan, C. in Houston, Colleen Guidetti, Don D., Dougal McS., Fin James, Fran Tomlin, Greg M., Jeannie Pinto, Jennie H., Joy R., Judy Myers, Julie Calliss, Kate Duncan, Kerry Toth, Leigh White, L.M.R., Lois Wagner, Manon-Camille, Maria

Bowes, Mariella F., Marika J., Mehul Raina, Nathan Castle, OP, N.W., Patrea O'Donoghue, Prisha, Radhika, Sach T., Sahil Raina, Sara, Sarah, Sher'ee Furtak-Ellis, Susanne Pearce, Susie Dolling, Sylvia Holzapfel, Tammy N., Tony Bacon, Trenna, Tricia Locke, T.S., Veathika Jain, Zoe Mac.

_◌

Production Team

To editor and indexer Theresa Duran (**duraneditorial.com**) for her humor, allergy to error, and a trained eye that could just as well have been deployed in espionage; to Tessa Avila (**tessaavila.com**) for her beautiful interior design that blends whimsy and substance; to Shruti Diwan (**shrutidiwan.com**) for her captivating cover design and aesthetic talent; to Sally Jaquet (**blaqjaqdesign.com**) for her InDesign wizardry.

_◌

Acknowledgment of Trademarks and Copyright

The author and publisher thank these entities and recognize rightful ownership of the following logos and trademarks to their respective owners: Apple Blossom perfume, Canadian Broadcasting Corporation, Facebook, Goodwill, Google and Google Maps, Instagram, Land Rover, Messenger, Mercedes-Benz, National Public Radio, Old Spice, Oprah/OWN, *Ripley's Believe It or Not*, *Sesame Street* and Sesame Workshop, Sony, Soul Publishing, Telstra Women in Business Awards, Triumph, and Tupperware.

We also recognize rightful ownership of the following song and film titles to their respective owners: *Analyze This* (1999 film); *City of Angels* (1998 film); *The Girl from Petrovka* (1974 film); "Danny Boy," written by Frederic Weatherly; "Fields of Gold," written and sung by Sting and later recorded by Eva Cassidy; "Lemon Tree," sung by The Seekers; "Shout," sung by Johnny O'Keefe; "Twist and Shout," sung by The Beatles; "What A Wonderful World," sung by Louis Armstrong; and "You Are My Sunshine," sung by Jimmie Davis.

About the Author

On paper, Alicia Young is a swirling mass of contradictions.

She is a one-time go-go dancer who has lived in a convent. She is both child-free and a mother (as an egg donor, she has biological children). And despite being Anglo-Indian, she cannot handle hot curry.

Alicia has contributed to newsrooms around the world as an anchor, foreign correspondent, and producer. She has worked with Walter Cronkite—and was suitably terrified.

Alicia was once told off by Mother Teresa for not having children (she forgot). She has volunteered at a leprosy hospital in India, an orphanage in Indonesia, and a seniors' home in Chile.

The Jam Jar Factor: At home, Alicia serves water only in jam jars—to honor a woman she met at age seven. This lady's home was sparse, and her threadbare furniture threatened to collapse under the weight of a child. Yet when she offered her guests a cold drink on a steaming day, she did so with uncommon hospitality. Alicia's parents, in turn, received those jam jars with quiet grace. It was an unspoken lesson in giving and receiving that remains vivid decades later.

In her spare time, Alicia handles parasols and power tools with equal ease (not really, but she helpfully holds the flashlight when needed).

Divinely Align Me is her seventh title.

Speaking Engagements

Alicia is a dynamic and engaging speaker, drawing on her global travel and background in television and radio news to weave a story around a range of topics. She welcomes inquiries for speaking opportunities throughout Australia, the US, and around the world.

Orders and Bulk Purchases

Divinely Align Me is available as both an ebook and a softcover on Amazon and other platforms. For bulk orders of any of Alicia's titles, please email info@aliciayoung.net. Bulk purchases are available to groups and organizations as gifts to their members or event attendees. Copies can also be purchased wholesale to raise both funds and awareness.

Contact

Parasol Press
PO Box 7029, Hutt Street, South Australia 5000
AUSTRALIA
info@aliciayoung.net

Social Media

Facebook and Instagram: **@authoraliciayoung**
Twitter: **@IamAliciaYoung**

A Request

If you're like me, you scribble in the margins of your books and highlight passages. (If you did that this time, I'm thrilled.) If you're a neater reader, please consider donating this copy to a public library, or slipping it into one of those charming free libraries. Buying books can be expensive, and you would be helping someone with your gift (a wonderful idea inspired by author Rob Schwartz).

Please consider a brief review on Amazon or post one to your favorite social media sites. I will, of course, owe you:

a) fine wine

b) Belgian chocolate

c) the kidney of your choice

Okay, I can't actually do that, but think of the karma!

Do You Have a Story for Me?

Messages of love, reassurance, and inspiration. Signs from angels and loved ones in spirit. Acts of kindness, whether minor or transformative . . .

I could soak in these stories all day. If one afternoon you find this book, dog-eared and yellowed with age, get in touch. If you spot a copy waterlogged on a park bench, email me. There is no expiration date; I will always welcome a note from you.

Warmly,

Alicia

info@aliciayoung.net

The 12 Stamps Project™

(BECAUSE WE'RE MORE LOGGED ON THAN EVER, BUT LESS CONNECTED)

The 12 Stamps Project™ taps the power of the hand-written word and boosts literacy. It's vital in this digital age, when it seems we're surgically attached to our screens. Someone in your life needs to hear from you; rediscover the impact of a card or letter on others.

Buy twelve stamps and commit to sending twelve notes this year. Jot a few lines to someone whose advice or practical help made a difference, whether yesterday or in your childhood. Comfort someone who is navigating change, loneliness, or the stress of a job hunt. Share a joke, a quirky observation, or a passionate opinion.

How Do I Get Started?

All it takes is the stamps, paper, and a few minutes. Some people start a small group at work, their after-school club, or sorority, while others distribute the stamps among family members.

An easy way to make a child feel important? Send them mail! Write to your niece, nephew, or teen cousin. Tell them that you've noticed how well they share, or the confident reader they've become, or how much they'll love college. We've seen everyone from first graders to professional athletes swell with pride. And a child or teen who receives a letter is more likely to write one; this is a powerful life skill for everything from a thank-you note to a job application.

Do you recall a special note that boosted you? Maybe it celebrated a milestone or a small act that still resonates for you. Share your ideas **@12stamps**—we'd love to hear from you!

Visit from Heaven

A SOUL'S MESSAGE OF LOVE, LOSS & FAMILY

You're about to be taken to the Other Side.
Your guide? The soul of a little boy.

Journalist and award-winning author Alicia Young recounts a transformative out-of-body experience in which she was visited by the spirit of an unborn child. Determined to convey a message of love to his grieving parents, "Bobby" reveals, through cinematic images, his own role in planning the circumstances of his brief life—and his past lives. Join them as he vividly:

- Consults wise, compassionate beings as he designs his soul plan
- Describes the power and freedom we have to choose our families
- Explains why he ultimately chose not to stay here on earth

This poignant account will help you to:

- Ease your heartache for a loved one who has passed
- Dissolve your fears around death—and witness the wonders of the Other Side
- Release thoughts of "Why me?" and gain rich insights into life's struggles

Get ready to embrace the magnificence of your own soul.

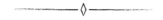

For more information about this award-winning title, visit
aliciayoung.net.

The Mother Teresa Effect

WHAT I LEARNED VOLUNTEERING FOR A SAINT

What's it like to meet a future saint?
To work for one?

Mother Teresa's mission to the poor resonated through every country, faith, income level, and worldview. Her compassion touched everyone from small children to heads of state—and one garden-variety Catholic.

Journalist Alicia Young volunteered in Calcutta (now Kolkata) over Mother's final Christmas in 1996. She divided her time between Kalighat, the Home for the Dying Destitute, and a rural leprosy hospital. In *The Mother Teresa Effect*, she narrates her transformative journey with humanity, color, and gentle humor.

As the world celebrates the newly canonized Saint Teresa, Alicia vividly:

- Reveals meeting her—an encounter that veered into unexpected territory
- Recounts daily life at the hospice and leprosy ward
- Explains how a one-time go-go dancer coped with living in a convent
- Chronicles daily life in Calcutta, from pavement dwellers to elegant soirees
- Relates anecdotes from others who have felt Saint Teresa's ripple effect
- Shares simple, potent lessons she learned on gratitude and nonjudgment

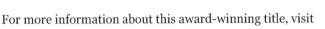

For more information about this award-winning title, visit
aliciayoung.net.

Two Eggs, Two Kids

AN EGG DONOR'S ACCOUNT OF FRIENDSHIP, INFERTILITY & SECRETS

Alicia Young doesn't have kids. (She forgot.)
Yet she has two biological children.

Two Eggs, Two Kids shares how Alicia came to donate her eggs to two couples—both good friends. The way these families began and unfolded are starkly different. One baby's origins were celebrated in the open; the other's, cloaked in secrecy.

Discover a touching and gently humorous look into the world of infertility, experienced by one in eight couples today. Meet:

- Alicia, the egg donor, who explains why she did it—and how
- Angela, one of the egg recipients, who recounts her journey
- Rachael, Angela's daughter, who discusses her "spare mom"

A Guided Tour to Being an Egg Donor:

- What to expect: the physical and emotional assessment
- Questions for donors/recipients and tips for friends
- Anecdotes from donors, recipients, and family members

An easy read for a potential egg donor, recipient, or their family/friends.
—Lynn Westphal, MD, FACOG, Stanford University Medical Center

A real, conversational account . . . insightful and thought provoking.
—Lauren Haring, RN, Director of Nursing, Genetics & IVF Institute
(givf.com)

A refreshing perspective on the journey to being an egg donor.
—Gail Sexton Anderson, EdM, Founder, Donor Concierge
(donorconcierge.com)

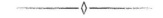

For more information about this award-winning title, visit
aliciayoung.net.

The Savvy Bride's Guide

SIMPLE WAYS TO A STYLISH & GRACEFUL WEDDING

Be a Savvy Bride!

Who gets a marriage proposal in the middle of a job interview? Alicia Young did. *Really.*

Then she nearly derailed her own wedding when she got flustered with the vows. Gazing into the eyes of her handsome groom, Jon, she declared, "I, Alicia, take you, Father Patrick. . . ."

She had almost married the priest.

While ring shopping, she breezily remarked, "Studies show, the bigger the diamond, the stronger the marriage." Jon didn't buy it (literally or figuratively). But years later, they're still happily married—even without a rock the size of an ice cube.

Tips and Tales from around the World!

The Savvy Bride's Guide: Simple Ways to a Stylish & Graceful Wedding will help you:
- Trim the guest list, control your budget, and still enjoy a decadent celebration.
- Speak fluent "bride," from *boutonnières* to *bomboniere*.
- Sort the key elements, solve the little details, and surprise your parents with heartfelt touches they will cherish.
- Handle family dynamics with the polish of a seasoned diplomat.

See also *The Savvy Bride's Guide: Your Wedding Checklist* for a handy countdown to the final three months.

———◊———

For more information about this award-winning title, visit **aliciayoung.net**.

The Savvy Bride's Guide

YOUR WEDDING CHECKLIST

The Countdown Is On: You're Getting Married!

The dress! The vows! The honeymoon! Now you're counting the sleeps until you glide down the aisle, a vision to behold. Everything is set for your big day, right?

Well, almost.

Building on *The Savvy Bride's Guide: Simple Ways to a Stylish & Graceful Wedding,* this checklist will steer you through these last few months, when cheerful chaos can bubble over into stress.

Tips from Savvy Brides around the World!

The Savvy Bride's Guide: Your Wedding Checklist will help you:

- Roll with late changes.
- Track RSVPs.
- Sort last-minute honeymoon tasks.
- Pen stylish, easy thank-you notes.
- Keep your sense of humor and make time for each other.
- Reflect on this new chapter of your life.
- Record journal entries and store keepsakes.

——————— ◊ ———————

For more information about this award-winning title, visit
aliciayoung.net.

The Savvy Girl's Guide to Grace

SMALL TOUCHES WITH BIG IMPACT— AT HOME, WORK & IN LOVE

Whatever happened to grace?

Perhaps it was the woman who texted through a funeral. Or the girl on the subway, who loudly recounted a drunken hook-up. Or the colleague who chatted between restroom stalls. Have you wondered: *"Whatever happened to grace?"* Does it really exist only in black-and-white movies? Frozen in time?

The Savvy Girl's Guide to Grace is a gentle, inner-beauty makeover for anyone who feels rushed. It's about living gracefully in our fast-paced, high-tech world—with humor and anecdotes from your fellow Savvy Girls.

Tap your inner Audrey Hepburn!

This is not a book about fish forks, napkins, or how to introduce a duchess and a count. It's about tapping our natural elegance to live a more beautiful life.

From college girls to career veterans, whether with family or friends, this book will help you to:

- Live a more savvy, graceful life—and spark a ripple effect in others.
- Transform your relationships with simple, thoughtful gestures.
- Show the world your best self—at work, on vacation, or with a date.
- See that grace is a powerful tool—far beyond being "nice."

———————— ◊ ————————

For more information about this award-winning title, visit **aliciayoung.net**.

Index

Printed in Great Britain
by Amazon

17834540R00130